Preface

Thank you for checking out my GR0568 and GR9768 solutions. It was a pleasure to write this booklet, and I hope you find my solutions to be a useful resource.

I have been put in an exceptional position to write these solutions. My time studying at Berkeley has proven to be more than enough training to answer the more advanced questions. However, what makes me uniquely qualified is my experience as a tutor; I work with students studying College Algebra, Calculus, and Linear Algebra every day, so remembering the necessary information was not an issue, and my work has given me experience explaining concepts to students.

The purpose of this text is simple: It's to help students study. This booklet is intended to have enough detail to help struggling students understand key concepts, but the design is such that it is also useful as a reference. All of the major theorems are mentioned, either within the main text, the glossary, or both. In particular, I took great pains to include theorems from Calculus and below, because it has probably been a long time for most of you. Everything is written from an intuitive perspective, and very few proofs are contained within the text.

Time management is an important aspect of the GRE test, and being mindful of the time constraints while you study is important. The test has 66 questions and you'll have 170 minutes to complete them, which means you have about two and a half minutes per problem. The techniques used here should be viable given those time constraints, though more detail is shown than necessary. However, no one is more qualified than you to optimize your time management system. You want to know how long it takes you to complete mathematical tasks with accuracy, when it would be best to skip or give up on a problem, and when it's best to push through and get one done. Please keep this in mind as you read the solutions, and frequently time yourself as you work through problems.

Good resources for test takers include the following. *Cracking the GRE Mathematics Subject Test* is probably the best resource for most students. The questions are very similar to those on the GRE, and it has very well done chapters that explain what you need to know and each one contains a little mini-test at the end to make sure you know the material. But *Cracking the GRE Mathematics Subject Test* does have some issues; problems are a little easier than would be ideal, and there is only one full-length practice test. My friend Charlie's *2012 UCLA GRE Workshop* has some great material as well, though a lot of it is more the best of other resources. You can view his practice problems at `http://www.math.ucla.edu/~cmarshak/GREWorkshop.html`. Charlie's page includes the GR0568 and GR9768 questions, which I did not include in this text due to copyright issues. The REA book *GRE Mathematics* is also good, mainly due to its difficulty, but the authors weren't able to emulate the actual GRE test as closely as the other sources I cited.

A plethora of resources were utilized while crafting this booklet. Wikipedia was extensively used for theorems; sometimes whole theorems were simply copied and pasted into this document with only minor changes. When this was done, a link in the glossary to the original theorem was included. Rudin's *Principles of Mathematical Analysis*, Stewart's *Calculus*, *Schaum's Outline of Discrete Mathematics* by Lipschutz and Lipson, and *Counter Examples in Analysis* by Gelbaum and Olmsted were all invaluable to me, and I recommend them all as study material if the GRE study guides aren't enough for you. It was also helpful to look at solutions posted on the *Math Stack Exchange*. And the *LaTeX Stack Exchange* was of great utility for information about LaTeX.

My apologies for any errors. Alas, one of the problems with self-published material is that it's often not feasible to hire editors.

And I must admit that I'm not the most careful writer. I welcome your help: If you find errors or have questions feel free to email me at `charles.tutoring@gmail.com`. So far your feedback has really helped improve the solutions. In particular, you guys found about half a dozen errors in the text, which have all been fixed so they won't confuse future readers. Keep it coming! It has been a pleasure to hear from you all.

To take care of a bit of shop work: For details about my tutoring business check out my website `http://www.rambotutoring.com`. I tutor throughout north San Diego county. At some point in time, I plan to write solutions to the other two public GRE math subject tests. The cover art was done by Rick (shadowthh2142 at *Deviant Art*). I tried to contact Rick directly to get explicit permission to use his art, but never got a response. However, he indicated on the *Deviant Art* website that it can be used as long as attribution is given.

Lastly, at the risk of sounding patronizing, I hope you enjoy studying for the GRE. Taking a standardized test is a high pressure ordeal, and students are often preoccupied with what comes after the test. But the problems tend to be well done, and questions are designed to be more about finding clever approaches than about relying on heavy memorization or computation. That's a good thing. And as a general tip, life is more enjoyable if you take the time to appreciate the things you're doing in the moment.

Good luck on the GRE!

Charles Rambo,
Escondido, California
June 2014

Chapter 1

GRE mathematics subject test GR0568 solutions

Question 1.1. ⎯⎯⎯⎯⎯⎯⎯⎯⎯⎯⎯⎯⎯⎯⎯⎯⎯⎯⎯⎯⎯⎯⎯
The *arc length* from $t = a$ to $t = b$, where x and y are functions of a parameter t, is

$$s = \int_a^b \sqrt{\left(\frac{dx}{dt}\right)^2 + \left(\frac{dy}{dt}\right)^2}\ dt.$$

Let's find the pieces

$$x = \cos t \quad \text{implies} \quad \frac{dx}{dt} = -\sin t$$

and

$$y = \sin t \quad \text{implies} \quad \frac{dy}{dt} = \cos t.$$

It follows that

$$s = \int_0^\pi \sqrt{\left(-\sin t\right)^2 + \left(\cos t\right)^2} \, dt$$

$$= \int_0^\pi \sqrt{\sin^2 t + \cos^2 t} \, dt$$

$$= \int_0^\pi dt$$

$$= \pi.$$

$\square$

Question 1.2. ———————————————————————
To find a tangent line, we need a point on the graph of y and the slope at that point. First, we find the point. When $x = 0$, $y = 0 + e^0 = 1$. Hence, the graph contains $(0, 1)$. Next, we find the slope. The derivative $y' = 1 + e^x$ gives the slope of the curve at x. It follows that when $x = 0$ the slope of our curve is $y' = 1 + e^0 = 2$. Thus, the equation of the tangent line is $y - 1 = 2(x - 1)$. Simplifying yields $y = 2x + 1$. $\square$

Question 1.3. ———————————————————————
Recall that the dimension of a vector space (or subspace) is defined to be the minimum number of elements that span the space, i.e. the number elements in a *basis* of the vector space. We can extend a basis of $V \cap W$ to a basis for either V or W, so the set of basis elements of $V \cap W$ must be a subset of a basis of both V and W. So $V \cap W$ can have at most 2 basis elements (this case corresponds to $V = W$) and a minimum of 0 elements (corresponding to the case where V and W are disjoint except for the zero vector). Of course, 1 basis element is also a possibility. $\square$

2

Question 1.4. ───────────────────────────────

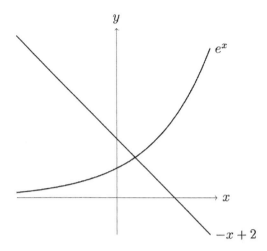

We break the expression $e^x - (-x + 2)$ into two parts $-x + 2$ and e^x, and consider where they intersect. Using basic graphing techniques, it's clear that there is exactly one point of intersection. Hence, $e^x + x - 2$ only has one zero.

From here onward, it's just a matter of finding where our zero lies. We will show our zero is in $[0, 1]$ using the *Intermediate value theorem*. Let $f(x) := e^x + x - 2 = e^x - (-x + 2)$. The function f is real-valued and continuous. It's clear that $f(0) = -1$ and $f(1) = e - 1 \approx 1.7$. So there must be a c in $[0, 1]$ such that $f(c) = 0$. □

Question 1.5. ───────────────────────────────
Since the coefficient in front of x^2 is 3 and the vertex of f is $(2, 0)$, it follows that $f(x) = 3(x - 2)^2$. If you're not familiar with vertex form, then consider the following argument. It's clear $f(2) = 2b + 24 = 0$, which implies $b = -12$. Either way, it follows that $f(5) = 3(5 - 2)^2 = 3(9) = 27$. □

Question 1.6. ——————————————————————————————————————

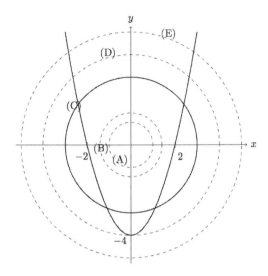

By drawing a picture, we see there are at most 4 places where a circle centered at $(0,0)$ will intersect the parabola. If we want all 4 intersections, the radius of our circle must be less than 4; if it's equal to 4, then it intersects the parabola at 3 points and if its radius is greater than 4 it intersects the parabola at 2 places. Furthermore, the radius must be greater than or equal to 2, because the circle doesn't intersect the parabola at all if its radius is less than 2. Answer (C) is the only equation satisfying all of our criteria because its radius is 3. $\qquad\square$

Question 1.7. ────────────────────────────────

It's clear $|x + 1| = \begin{cases} x + 1, & \text{if } x \geq -1 \\ -(x + 1), & \text{if } x < -1 \end{cases}$. So,

$$\int_{-1}^{3} |x + 1| \; dx = \int_{-1}^{3} x + 1 \; dx + \int_{-3}^{-1} -(x + 1) \; dx$$

$$= \int_{-1}^{3} x + 1 \; dx - \int_{-3}^{-1} x + 1 \; dx$$

$$= \frac{x^2}{2} + x \Big|_{-1}^{3} - \left(\frac{x^2}{2} + x \right) \Big|_{-3}^{-1}$$

$$= \frac{9}{2} + 3 - \left(\frac{1}{2} - 1 \right) - \left(\frac{1}{2} - 1 \right) + \left(\frac{9}{2} - 3 \right)$$

$$= 10.$$

□

Question 1.8. ────────────────────────────────

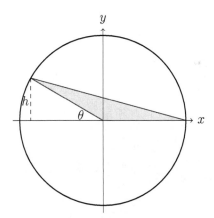

Without loss of generality, we can assume one side of our triangle on the positive x-axis. Let h and θ be as shown in the picture. Due to symmetry, we need only consider values of θ between 0 and

180°. In this interval, it's clear $h = \sin \theta$.

From Geometry, we know the area A of our triangle is

$$A = \frac{1}{2} \cdot 1 \cdot h$$
$$= \frac{\sin \theta}{2}.$$

The maximum value of $\sin \theta$, for θ between 0 and 180°, is 1, so the maximum value of A must be $1/2$. $\qquad\square$

Question 1.9. ────────────────────────────
Because $x^8 < x^4$ when $0 < x < 1$, it's clear $\sqrt{1 - x^4} \leq \sqrt{1 - x^8} \leq 1 \leq \sqrt{1 + x^4}$ for $0 \leq x \leq 1$, where the inequality is strict except at $x = 0$ and 1. Therefore, due to basic *integration properties*,

$$\int_0^1 \sqrt{1 - x^4} \, dx < \int_0^1 \sqrt{1 - x^8} \, dx < 1 < \int_0^1 \sqrt{1 + x^4} \, dx.$$

$\qquad\square$

Question 1.10. ────────────────────────────
This is a simple application of the *first derivative test*. Our critical numbers are 2 and 5. Let's make a table to see where g is increasing and decreasing:

Intervals	$(-\infty, 2)$	$(2, 5)$	$(5, \infty)$
Test numbers	1	3	6
$g'(x)$	$g'(1) > 0$	$g'(3) < 0$	$g'(6) > 0$
g Increasing/Decreasing	Increasing	Decreasing	Increasing

We can eliminate (A), (C), (D), and (E). The number $g(1)$ is nothing special, since g keeps increasing until 2. Neither $g(3)$ nor $g(4)$ is a relative extreme, since g is decreasing between 2 and 5. And $g(5)$ is a relative minimum.

The first derivative test tells us that the value $g(2)$ is a relative maxima. Hence, it must be the largest by the process of elimination. $\qquad\square$

Question 1.11. ──────────────────────────────────

It's not too hard to see that the number 15 and 26.6 are close to the perfect squares 16 and 25, respectively, so let's modify $\sqrt{1.5}(266)^{3/2}$ a bit to get 15 and 26.6 inside the square roots and then substitute as needed. It's clear

$$\sqrt{1.5}(266)^{3/2} = \sqrt{\frac{15}{10}}(26.6 \cdot 10)^{3/2}$$
$$= 10\sqrt{15}(26.6)^{3/2}$$
$$\approx 10\sqrt{16}(25)^{3/2}$$
$$= 10 \cdot 4 \cdot 125$$
$$= 5\,000$$

This is an underestimate since the squareroot reduces the difference between 16 and 15 and the $3/2$ power increases the difference between 25 and 26.6. So now is a good time to select (E) during testing.

But we're not being timed (now), so let's look at how much error we're talking about. Define $f(x, y) := 10\sqrt{x}y^{3/2}$. We know from Calculus that $f(15, 26.6) - f(16, 25) \approx df = f_x(16, 25)dx + f_y(16, 25)dy$, where f_x and f_y are the partial derivatives with respect to x and y, respectively. Evaluating we get $f_x(16, 25) = 5(25)^{3/2}/\sqrt{16} = 156.25$ and $f_y(16, 25) = 15\sqrt{15 \cdot 25} = 300$. It follows that $f(15, 26.6) - f(16, 25) \approx 156.25(-1) + 300(1.6) = 323.75$, which implies $f(15, 26.6) \approx 5\,323.75$. Using a calculator, we see that $f(15, 26.6) = 5\,313.34\ldots$. ☐

Question 1.12. ──────────────────────────────────

It's clear A is of the form $\begin{pmatrix} a & b \\ b & a \end{pmatrix}$, where $a+b = k$. Thus $A\begin{pmatrix} 1 \\ 0 \end{pmatrix} = \begin{pmatrix} a \\ b \end{pmatrix}$, $A\begin{pmatrix} 0 \\ 1 \end{pmatrix} = \begin{pmatrix} b \\ a \end{pmatrix}$, and $A\begin{pmatrix} 1 \\ 1 \end{pmatrix} = \begin{pmatrix} a+b \\ a+b \end{pmatrix} = \begin{pmatrix} k \\ k \end{pmatrix} = k\begin{pmatrix} 1 \\ 1 \end{pmatrix}$. So $\begin{pmatrix} 1 \\ 1 \end{pmatrix}$ is the only eigenvector listed. ☐

Question 1.13. ─────────────────────────────────────
Let the area in the yard be $A := \ell w$, where ℓ is the length and w is the width of the yard. By hypothesis, $\ell + 2w = x$. Using substitution, it follows that $A = (x - 2w)w = xw - 2w^2$. Hence, $dA/dw = x - 4w$. Letting $dA/dw = 0$ and solving for w yields $w = x/4$. Because this is a parabola with a negative coefficient in front of the w^2 term, this critical number maximizes A. Thus, $A(x/4) = (x - 2x/4)x/4 = x^2/8$ is the maximum area. □

Question 1.14. ─────────────────────────────────────
This problem is equivalent to finding

$$7^{25} \pmod{10}.$$

All that's left is an easy computation:

$$
\begin{aligned}
7^{25} &\equiv 7^{24} \cdot 7 \\
&\equiv 49^{12} \cdot 7 \\
&\equiv 9^{12} \cdot 7 \\
&\equiv 81^6 \cdot 7 \\
&\equiv 1^6 \cdot 7 \\
&\equiv 7 \pmod{10}.
\end{aligned}
$$

□

Question 1.15. ─────────────────────────────────────
Let's go through the ones that are not necessarily true first. It's not (A), because $[-2, 3]$ is *compact* and its image under a continuous map is compact, and by the *Heine-Borel theorem* every compact space is bounded. Since f in continuous over the interval $[-2, 3]$, the integral must exist, that means it can't be (B). Choice (C) is the *Intermediate value theorem*, and (D) is the integral form of the *mean value theorem*.

By the process of elimination, it must be (E). And we can be confident about our choice, because

$$\lim_{h \to 0} \frac{f(h) - f(0)}{h} =: f'(0),$$

which need not exist because differentiability is a stronger property than continuity. Consider $f(x) = |x|$; f isn't differentiable at 0, though it is continuous and real-valued on $[-2, 3]$. □

Question 1.16. ──

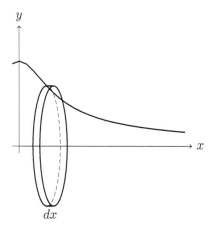

The first step is to find a formula for an infinitesimal chunk volume dV. At the point $(x, 1/\sqrt{1+x^2})$, the cross section perpendicular to the xy-plane is a disk of radius $1/\sqrt{1+x^2}$, so its area must be

$$\pi \left(\frac{1}{\sqrt{1+x^2}} \right)^2 = \frac{\pi}{1+x^2}.$$

It follows that

$$dV = \frac{\pi}{1+x^2} \, dx,$$

where dx is an infinitesimal horizontal length parallel to the x-axis. The volume of the generated solid is simply the infinite sum of these infinitesimal chunks dV for all $x \geq 0$ (i.e. $V = \int_{x \geq 0} dV$). Hence,

$$V = \int_0^\infty \frac{\pi}{1 + x^2} \, dx$$

$$= \pi \text{Arctan } x \, \Big|_0^\infty$$

$$= \pi \left(\lim_{t \to \infty} \text{Arctan } t - \text{Arctan } 0 \right)$$

$$= \pi \left(\frac{\pi}{2} - 0 \right)$$

$$= \frac{\pi^2}{2}.$$

A list of *antiderivatives* is contained in the glossary. □

Question 1.17.

We use *Descartes's rule of signs*, which says:

> Suppose $f(x) = a_n x^n + a_{n-1} x^{n-1} + \ldots + a_1 x + a_0$. Then the number of positive zeros of f is equal to the number of sign changes of $f(x)$ or is an even number less. Furthermore, the number of negative zeros of f is equal to the number of sign changes of $f(-x)$ or is an even number less.

Since there is one sign change in $2x^5 + 8x - 7$, Descartes's rule of signs implies $2x^5 + 8x - 7$ has one positive zero. To find the negative zeros, consider $2(-x)^5 + 8(-x) - 7 = -2x^5 - 8x - 7$. There are no sign changes so there are no negative zeros. Thus $2x^5 + 8x - 7$ has one real zero. □

Question 1.18.

Recall that the nullity of T and the rank of T are defined to be the dimensions of the null space and the image, respectively. Since $\{v \in V : T(v) = 0\}$ is the definition of the null space, all we need to do is collect the pieces and apply the *rank nullity theorem*. The dimension of V is 6, and the dimension of W is 4. Since T is onto, the dimension of the rank must be the same as the dimension of the codomain, i.e. the rank must be 4. It follows that $n + 4 = 6$, where n is the dimension of the null space. Thus, $n = 2$. □

Question 1.19. ————————————————————————
Due to elementary *integration properties,*

$$\int_0^x f'(t)\, dt > \int_0^x g'(t)\, dt$$

because $f'(x) > g'(x)$ for $x > 0$. Thus, the *Fundamental theorem of Calculus* implies that

$$f(x) - f(0) > g(x) - g(0).$$

$\square$

Question 1.20. ————————————————————————
Let $\{q_n\}$ be a sequence of rational numbers such that $q_n \to y$ as $n \to \infty$, and let $\{x_n\}$ be a sequence of irrationals such that $x_n \to y$ as $n \to \infty$. If f is continuous at y, then $f(q_n) \to y/2$ and $f(x_n) \to y/3$. But $\lim_{x \to y} f(x)$ cannot equal two different values if f is continuous at y, so we need $y/2 = y/3$. This can only occur when $y = 0$. It follows that f is discontinuous everywhere except 0. $\square$

Question 1.21. ————————————————————————
The set $P_{12} \cap P_{20} = \{60\}$ is nonempty because $12 \cdot 5 = 20 \cdot 3$.

Let's spend a bit of time thinking about the general rule. Suppose $P_m \cap P_n$ is nonempty and $m \neq n$. Then there must be primes p and q such that $m \cdot p = n \cdot q$. When this is the case, m and n share all but one prime factor; m has one more factor of q than n, and n has one more factor of p than m. In our case, 12 has one more factor of 3 than 20, and 20 has one more factor of 5 than 12. $\square$

Question 1.22. ————————————————————————
It's clear that I and II are subspaces, but III isn't because it's not closed under scalar addition (among other reasons). Suppose h is in

$$\{h : h''(x) = h(x) + 1 \text{ for all } x\},$$

and let r be in $\mathbb{R}$. Then $h''(x) = h(x) + 1$, or $h(x) = h'(x) - 1$. It follows that $rh(x) = rh''(x) + r \neq rh''(x) + 1$ for $r \neq 1$.

Let's take the time to check the subspace axioms for I and II, since we're not on the clock.

First, I:

Closed under addition: Suppose f_1 and f_2 are in $\{f : f''(x) - 2f'(x) + 3f(x) = 0$ for all $x\}$. Then $f_1(x) = \frac{1}{3}[f_1''(x) - 2f_1'(x)]$ and $f_2(x) = \frac{1}{3}[f_2'(x) - 2f_2'(x)]$. So,

$$(f_1 + f_2)(x) = f_1(x) + f_2(x)$$
$$= \frac{1}{3}[f_1''(x) - 2f_1'(x)] + \frac{1}{3}[f_2'(x) - 2f_2'(x)]$$
$$= \frac{1}{3}[(f_1 + f_2)''(x) - 2(f_1 + f_2)(x)],$$

which is in our subspace.

Closed under scalar multiplication: Let r be in $\mathbb{R}$ and f be in $\{f : f$ is twice differentiable and $f''(x) - 2f'(x) + 3f(x) = 0$ for all $x\}$. Then

$$(rf)(x) = rf(x)$$
$$= \frac{1}{3}[rf''(x) - 2rf'(x)]$$
$$= \frac{1}{3}[(rf)''(x) - 2(rf)'(x)],$$

which in in our subspace.

Contains the zero vector: Consider the zero function $O(x) := 0$. It's clear $O(x) = \frac{1}{3}[O''(x) - 2O'(x)] = 0$, and $(f + O)(x) = (O + f)(x) = f(x)$.

Now, II:

Closed under addition: Suppose g_1 and g_2 are in $\{g : g''(x) = 3g'(x)$ for all $x\}$. Then

$$(g_1 + g_2)''(x) = g_1''(x) + g_2''(x)$$
$$= 3g_1'(x) + 3g_2'(x)$$
$$= 3(g_1 + g_2)'.$$

Closed under scalar multiplication: Suppose g is in $\{g : g''(x) = 3g'(x)$ for all $x\}$. Then $(rg)''(x) = rg''(x) = 3(rg)'(x)$.

Contains the zero vector: It's the same zero vector $O(x) := 0$ as I, and it's just as easy to prove $O(x)$ is in $\{g : g''(x) = 3g'(x)$ for all $x\}$.

$\square$

Question 1.23.
Let's relabel to avoid confusion. Define $f(x) := 10x$ and $g(x) := e^{bx}$. If f is tangent to g at $x = x_0$, then $f'(x_0) = g'(x_0)$, i.e. $10 = be^{bx_0}$. Solving for x_0 yields $x_0 = \log(10/b)/b$. To be tangent, we also need $f(x_0) = g(x_0)$, so

$$f\left(\frac{\log(10/b)}{b}\right) = \frac{10\log(10/b)}{b}$$
$$= g\left(\frac{\log(10/b)}{b}\right)$$
$$= e^{\log(10/b)}$$
$$= \frac{10}{b}.$$

That is, $10\log(10/b)/b = 10/b$ which implies $\log(10/b) = 1$. Using *logarithm properties* to change the equation to exponential form gives $10/b = e^1$. Therefore $b = 10/e$. $\square$

Question 1.24.
We could differentiate this now using the *Fundamental theorem of Calculus*, but let's try the direct approach:

$$h(x) = \int_0^{x^2} e^{x+t}\,dt$$
$$= e^{x+t}\Big|_{t=0}^{x^2}$$
$$= e^{x^2+x} - e^x.$$

Note: that x is fixed with respect to t, so x behaves like a constant when integrating with respect to t.

Now, we differentiate:

$$h'(x) = \frac{d}{dx}\left(e^{x^2+x} - e^x\right)$$
$$= (2x+1)e^{x^2+x} - e^x.$$

Thus, $h'(1) = (2+1)e^{1+1} - e = 3e^2 - e.$ □

Question 1.25.

Let's see what a_{30} looks like:

$$a_{30} = \frac{31}{29} \cdot \frac{30}{28} \cdot \frac{29}{27} \cdot \frac{28}{26} \cdot \ldots \cdot \frac{6}{4} \cdot \frac{5}{3} \cdot \frac{4}{2} \cdot \frac{3}{1} \cdot 1.$$

So the numerator in the n-th factor will cancel with the denominator in $(n+2)$-th factor most of the time. When won't this happen? Well, the numerators in the twenty-ninth and thirtieth factors won't cancel, because there are no thirty-first and thirty-second factors. Furthermore, since there is no -1-th factor and the rule doesn't hold for the first factor, the denominators in the second and third factors won't cancel either. With our cancelation rules in mind, we see

$$a_{30} = 31 \cdot 30 \cdot \frac{1}{2} = (15)(31).$$ □

Question 1.26.

Recall the *second derivatives test* from third semester Calculus:

Suppose that the function $f : \mathbb{R}^2 \to \mathbb{R}$ has continuous second order partial derivatives in some $E \subseteq \mathbb{R}^2$. Suppose the point (a,b) in E is a critical point, i.e. $f_x(a,b) = 0$ and $f_y(a,b) = 0$. Define

$$H_f(x,y) := \det \begin{pmatrix} f_{xx}(x,y) & f_{xy}(x,y) \\ f_{yx}(x,y) & f_{yy}(x,y) \end{pmatrix} =$$
$$f_{xx}(x,y)f_{yy}(x,y) - [f_{xy}(x,y)]^2.$$

Then

- if $f_{xx}(a, b) > 0$ and $H_f(a, b) > 0$, then $f(a, b)$ is a relative minimum;

- if $f_{xx}(a, b) < 0$ and $H_f(a, b) > 0$, then $f(a, b)$ is a relative maximum;

- if $H_f(a, b) < 0$, then (a, b) is a saddle point;

- if $H_f(a, b) = 0$, then the test gives no information.

Let's find our critical points. The partial derivative with respect to x and y are

$$f_x(x, y) = 2x - 2y \quad \text{and} \quad f_y(x, y) = -2x + 3y^2,$$

respectively. Our critical numbers occur when our first order partial derivates are zero, so let $2x - 2y = 0$ and $-2x + 3y^2 = 0$. The first equation implies that all extreme must lie on $x = y$ so we're ready to choose (A), but let's keep going.

We need the critical numbers. Using substitution and a bit of algebra on the equations $2x - 2y = 0$ and $-2x + 3y^2 = 0$, we conclude $3x^2 - 2x = x(3x - 2) = 0$. That means our critical numbers are $(0, 0)$ and $(2/3, 2/3)$.

Next, we find $H_f(x, y)$. The second order partial derivatives are:

$$f_{xx}(x, y) = 2, \quad f_{xy}(x, y) = f_{yx}(x, y) = -2,$$
$$\text{and} \quad f_{yy}(x, y) = 6y.$$

It follows that $H_f(x, y) = 12y - 4$.

With the second derivatives test in mind, we examine our critical points.

- $(0, 0)$: $H_f(0, 0) = -4 > 0$, so $(0, 0)$ is a saddle point;

- $(2/3, 2/3)$: $f_{xx}(2/3, 2/3) = 2 > 0$ and $H_f(2/3, 2/3) = 8 - 4 = 4 > 0$, so $f(2/3, 2/3)$ is relative minimum.

Obviously, theses results exclude (C), but could $(2/3, 2/3)$ be an absolute minimum? No. Why? Because f has no lower bound: fix x and you can see $f(x, y) = x^2 - 2xy + y^3 \to -\infty$ as $y \to -\infty$. $\square$

Question 1.27.

We will use simultaneous equations to solve this problem. Since most of our options have simple functions describing the x variable, we solve for x first.

$$-3(2x + y - 3z) = -6x - 3y + 9z$$
$$= 0$$

So,

$$
\begin{array}{r}
-6x \quad -3y \quad +9z \quad = 0 \\
+ \quad\quad x \quad +3y \quad -2z \quad =7 \\
\hline
-5x \quad\quad\quad\quad +7z \quad = 7,
\end{array}
$$

or $z = 1 + 5x/7$. To remove the fraction, let $x = 7t$. This implies $z = 1 + 5t$. We were given that $2x + y - 3z = 0$, so $y = -2x + 3z = -2(7t) + 3(1 + 5t) = t + 3$. Thus the solution is $\{(x, y, x) : x = 7t, y = 3 + t, z = 1 + 5t, t \in \mathbb{R}\}$. □

Question 1.28.

Let blue marks denote deletion of a side. The graph below satisfies the necessary criteria.

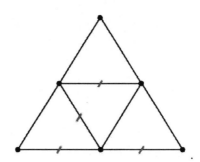

□

Question 1.29. ———————————————————————————

Let's find a counterexample to $e^f \sim e^g$. Consider $f(x) = x$ and $g(x) = x + 1$. It's clear $\lim\limits_{x \to \infty} \dfrac{f(x)}{g(x)} = 1$. But

$$\lim_{x \to \infty} \frac{e^x}{e^{x+1}} = \lim_{x \to \infty} \frac{1}{e}$$
$$= \frac{1}{e}$$
$$\neq 1.$$

This is enough to move on, but we're not being timed so let's verify that the others work.

First, $f^2 \sim g^2$.

$$\lim_{x \to \infty} \frac{\big(f(x)\big)^2}{\big(g(x)\big)^2} = \left(\lim_{x \to \infty} \frac{f(x)}{g(x)} \right)^2$$
$$= 1^2$$
$$= 1$$

Next, $\sqrt{f} \sim \sqrt{g}$. The argument is very similar.

$$\lim_{x \to \infty} \frac{\sqrt{f(x)}}{\sqrt{g(x)}} = \sqrt{\lim_{x \to \infty} \frac{f(x)}{g(x)}}$$
$$= \sqrt{1}$$
$$= 1$$

17

We continue by considering $f + g \sim 2g$.

$$\lim_{x \to \infty} \frac{f(x) + g(x)}{2g(x)} = \frac{1}{2} \lim_{x \to \infty} \frac{f(x)}{g(x)} + 1$$
$$= \frac{1}{2}(1 + 1)$$
$$= 1$$

Onto $g \sim f$.

$$\lim_{x \to \infty} \frac{g(x)}{f(x)} = \lim_{x \to \infty} \frac{1}{\frac{f(x)}{g(x)}}$$
$$= \frac{1}{\lim_{x \to \infty} \frac{f(x)}{g(x)}}$$
$$= \frac{1}{1}$$
$$= 1.$$

$\square$

Question 1.30. ————————————————————————
The negation of "f is one-to-one and onto Y" is "f is not one-to-one or f is not onto Y" (remember that "or" is inclusive). Statement R is "f is not one-to-one" and Q means f is onto, so not Q must mean f is not onto. We can conclude that R or not Q is the correct answer. $\square$

Question 1.31. ————————————————————————
It's easy to see that $dy/dx \to \infty$ as $|y| \to \infty$, which narrows our selection down to (A) and (B). Since $dy/dx > 0$, we exclude choice (B) because the derivative of that function is about 0 when its graph intersects the y-axis. $\square$

Question 1.32. ────────────────────────────────
We can immediately exclude property I, because it fails whenever $\odot$ is not commutative.

Property II follows. Consider

$$n(x \oplus y) = \underbrace{(x \oplus y) \oplus (x \oplus y) \oplus \cdots \oplus (x \oplus y)}_{n \text{ times}}$$
$$= \underbrace{(x \oplus x \oplus \cdots \oplus x)}_{n \text{ times}} \oplus \underbrace{(y \oplus y \cdots \oplus y)}_{n \text{ times}}$$
$$= nx \oplus ny.$$

Property III follows due to a similar argument.

$$x^n \odot x^m = \underbrace{(x \odot x \odot \cdots \odot x)}_{n \text{ times}} \odot \underbrace{(x \odot x \odot \cdots \odot x)}_{m \text{ times}}$$
$$= \underbrace{(x \odot x \odot \cdots \odot x)}_{n+m \text{ times}}$$
$$= x^{n+m}.$$

$\square$

Question 1.33. ────────────────────────────────
Let's go through the process. We plug in a = 273 and b = 110, and our first r = 273 mod 110 = 53. For the next step a = 110 and b = 53, so r = 110 mod 53 = 4. Then a = 53, b = 4, so r = 1. Then a = 4, b = 1, so r = 0. Thus, our sequence of r's is 53, 4, 1, 0. $\square$

Question 1.34. ────────────────────────────────
Since the line containing our points also contains the centers of the spheres, all we need to do is calculate the distance between the centers of the spheres, and subtract the two radii. The distance

between the centers of the spheres is

$$d = \sqrt{(-3-2)^2 + (2-1)^2 + (4-3)^2}$$
$$= \sqrt{25+1+1}$$
$$= 3\sqrt{3}.$$

The radius of the first sphere is 1, and the second's is 2. It follows that the distance, between the points closest to each other on the spheres is $3\sqrt{3} - 1 - 2 = 3(\sqrt{3} - 1)$. □

Question 1.35. ───
We will use the *Fundamental counting principle* extensively. First, the total number of permutations of men and women is 15!. To find the number of permutations where all the men are seated next to each other, consider the collection of men to be one unit, which gives us 10! permutations of the women and the "men-unit". Within the "men-unit", there are 6! ways to seat the group of men. It follows that there are a total of 10!6! ways to seat the group if all the men sit together. Thus, the probability that all the men will sit together is 10!6!/15!. □

Question 1.36. ───
All but (A) are claims equivalent to saying the columns of M are linearly independent. Recall M having linearly independent columns implies the only solution to $M\boldsymbol{x} = \boldsymbol{0}$ is $\boldsymbol{x} = \boldsymbol{0}$ (B), which implies every equation of the form $M\boldsymbol{x} = \boldsymbol{b}$ has only one solution (C), which implies that M is invertible (E), which implies that the determinant of M is nonzero (D).

To see why (A) isn't equivalent to the rest, consider

$$M = \begin{pmatrix} 1 & 0 & 0 & 0 & 1 \\ 0 & 1 & 0 & 0 & 1 \\ 0 & 0 & 1 & 0 & 1 \\ 0 & 0 & 0 & 1 & 1 \\ 0 & 0 & 0 & 0 & 0 \end{pmatrix}.$$

Clearly, the columns aren't linearly independent, though they are pairwise independent. □

20

Question 1.37. ────────────────────────────────

Let $z = x + iy$, where x and y are real numbers. Then $z^2 = (x + iy)^2 = x^2 - y^2 + 2ixy$ and $|z|^2 = x^2 + y^2$. It's clear this implies $y^2 = ixy$, but a real number can't equal an imaginary one, so $y = 0$. Thus the equation must describe a line. $\qquad\square$

Question 1.38. ────────────────────────────────

The definition of the set $f^{-1}(Y)$ is $\{x \in A : f(x) \in Y\}$, where $Y \subseteq B$. So it's clear that $C \subseteq f^{-1}(f(C))$ because x in C implies $f(x)$ in $f(C)$ so x in $f^{-1}(f(C))$. $\qquad\square$

Question 1.39. ────────────────────────────────

We use the *Law of cosines*. The identity states

$$c^2 = a^2 + b^2 - 2ab \cos C,$$

where a, b, and c are sides of a triangle and C is the angle opposite c.

In this situation the identity implies $s^2 = 1 + r^2 - 2r \cos 110°$, and taking square roots yields $s = \sqrt{1 + r^2 - 2r \cos 110°}$.

$$
\begin{aligned}
\lim_{\substack{s \to \infty \\ r \to \infty}} (s - r) &= \lim_{r \to \infty} \sqrt{1 + r^2 - 2r \cos 110°} - r \\
&= \lim_{r \to \infty} \frac{1 + r^2 - 2r \cos 110° - r^2}{\sqrt{1 + r^2 - 2r \cos 110°} + r} \\
&= \lim_{r \to \infty} \frac{1 - 2r \cos 110°}{\sqrt{1 + r^2 - 2r \cos 110°} + r} \\
&= \lim_{r \to \infty} \frac{\frac{1}{r} - 2 \cos 110°}{\sqrt{\frac{1}{r^2} + 1 - \frac{2 \cos 110°}{r}} + 1} \\
&= -\cos 110° \\
&= \cos 70°.
\end{aligned}
$$

In conclusion, $0 < \cos 70° < \cos 60° = 1/2 < 1$, so the solution must be (B). $\square$

Question 1.40.
Consider

$$f(x) := \begin{cases} 0, & \text{if } x \geq 1/2 \\ x - 1/2, & \text{if } x < 1/2 \end{cases} \quad \text{and}$$

$$g(x) := \begin{cases} x - 1/2, & \text{if } x \geq 1/2 \\ 0, & \text{if } x < 1/2. \end{cases}$$

It's clear that both of these functions are continuous on $[0,1]$ and real valued. It's also clear $(fg)(x) = 0$. $\square$

Question 1.41.
Green's theorem says that

$$\oint_C (2x - y)\ dx + (x + 3y)\ dy = \iint_{\{(x,y):\ x^2+y^2<1\}} \frac{\partial}{\partial x}(x + 3y)$$

$$- \frac{\partial}{\partial y}(2x - y)\ dA$$

$$= \iint_{\{(x,y):\ x^2+y^2<1\}} 1 + 1\ dA$$

$$= 2A$$

$$= 2\pi.$$

$\square$

Question 1.42. ————————————————————————
This is simply an application of a few *probability properties*. Consider the following argument.

$$
\begin{aligned}
P(X > 3 \text{ or } Y > 3) &= 1 - P(X \le 3 \text{ and } Y \le 3) \\
&= 1 - P(X \le 3) \cdot P(X \le 3) \\
&= 1 - \left(P(X \le 3) \right)^2 \\
&= 1 - \left(\frac{1}{2} + \frac{1}{4} + \frac{1}{8} \right)^2 \\
&= 1 - \frac{49}{64} \\
&= \frac{15}{64}.
\end{aligned}
$$

□

Question 1.43. ————————————————————————
Recall *Euler's formula*:

$$
e^{i\theta} = \cos\theta + i\sin\theta.
$$

In particular, we need that $e^{2\pi i} = 1$ and $e^{\pi i} = -1$.

Hence, $z^5 = 1$, which implies $z^5 - 1 = (z-1)(z^4 + z^3 + z^2 + z + 1) = 0$, since $z \ne 1$ we can divide both sides by $z - 1$, which gives us $z^4 + z^3 + z^2 + z + 1 = 0$. From here, it's only a matter of substitution and factorization.

$$1 + z^2 + z^3 + 5z^4 + 4z^5 + 4z^6 + 4z^7 + 4z^8 + 5z^9$$
$$= (1 + z^2 + z^3 + z^4) + 4z^4(1 + z + z^2$$
$$+ z^3 + z^4) + 5z^9$$
$$= 5z^9$$
$$= 5\left(e^{2\pi i/5}\right)^9$$
$$= 5e^{2\pi i}e^{8\pi i/5}$$
$$= 5e^{8\pi i/5}$$
$$= 5e^{\pi i}e^{3\pi i/5}$$
$$= 5(-1)e^{3\pi i/5}$$
$$= -5e^{3\pi/5}.$$

□

Question 1.44.

The probability distribution for the number of heads occurring on a fair coin is a *binomial distribution*. In general, for a binomial distribution:

- The expected value is $\mu = np$
- The standard deviation is $\sigma = \sqrt{np(1 - p)}$,

where n is the number of trials and p is the probability of the affirmative case. It's also helpful to note that for large n, the normal distribution is a good approximation of a binomial distribution.

Onto our problem. We were given that $n = 100$ and $p = 1/2$. So $\mu = 100(1/2) = 50$ and $\sigma = \sqrt{100(1/2)(1/2)} = 5$. Since the probability of obtaining any specific number of heads or tails is quite low, we exclude (A). As mentioned above, the normal distribution is a good approximation for the binomial distribution, so the probability $T \geq 60$ or $H \leq 40$ is low, because it's two standard deviations from the expected result of 50. As such, exclude (B). Exclude (E) because those results are even further away from the 50. We've narrowed it down to (C) and (D). Choice (D) is equivalent to stating $48 \leq H \leq 52$. So the events in (D) are a bit closer to the expected value of 50 than those in $51 \leq H \leq 55$. Therefore we conclude the solution is (D). □

Question 1.45.
This is a simple application of *pigeonhole principle*. However, we won't reference it directly in our argument.

Statement I is true. Since there will always be twenty-one points, less in one sector implies more in another. As such, to minimize the number of points in the sector with the most, we distribute the points as homogeneously as possible. So, we would want to put $21/5 = 4.2$ points in each sector, but this is impossible since we can't put 0.2 points in a sector. Thus the most homogenous distribution would have 5 points in one sector.

Statement II is a lie. The situation described in option I proves that II isn't necessarily true, since we could have 4 points in four sectors and 5 in the remaining sector.

Statement III is a legitimate proposition. Consider new sectors created by combining the adjacent sectors in the picture above. Each sector is adjacent to two others, so we double counted the old sectors. Therefore, we've also double counted the number of points, so our new sectors have a combined total of 42 points. There are a total of 5 new sectors. To minimize the number of points in the new sector with the most, we want to distribute the points as homogeneously as possible. That means we want to put $42/5 = 8.4$ points in each new sector. But the most we can put in any new sector is 8, so one new sector must contain an additional point. □

Question 1.46.
We need the following identity:

Let z be a complex number, and $|z|$ the modulus of z. Then $z = |z|e^{i\theta} = |z|(\cos\theta + i\sin\theta)$, for some θ.

Since the modulus of each element in G is 1, the above identity simplifies to $z = e^{i\theta}$.

Onto our problem. It's clear II follows from III. Choice III also implies I, because $z \mapsto \bar{z}$ is the same as $z \mapsto z^{-1}$ (since $z^{-1} = e^{-i\theta} =$

25

$\cos(-\theta) + i\sin(-\theta) = \cos\theta - i\sin\theta$). So all we need to do is prove III. The exponent rules for multiplication prove that $z \mapsto z^k$ will be a homomorphism. Because i generates the group, all that's left to show is that every map takes i to i^k for some integer k. Since $i = e^{i\pi/2}$, it's not too tough to see that $i \mapsto 1 = i^4$, $i \mapsto -1 = i^2$, $i \mapsto -i = i^3$, and $i \mapsto i = i^1$. $\qquad\square$

Question 1.47. ———————————————————————
We need the formula for *work* done.

Let $C := \{\gamma(t) : a \le t \le b\}$, where $\gamma : \mathbb{R} \to \mathbb{R}^3$ is a differentiable in each slot. Then the work done by a vector field $\boldsymbol{F}$ over C is

$$W = \int_C \boldsymbol{F} \cdot d\gamma = \int_a^b \boldsymbol{F} \cdot \gamma'(t)\, dt.$$

In our case, the formula above implies

$$W = \int\limits_{\{(t,t^2,t^3):\ 0 \le t \le 1\}} (-1,0,1) \cdot d\gamma$$

$$= \int_0^1 (-1,0,1) \cdot (1, 2t, 3t^2)\, dt$$

$$= \int_0^1 -1 + 3t^2\, dt$$

$$= -t + t^3 \Big|_0^1$$

$$= -1 + 1 - (0)$$

$$= 0.$$

$\qquad\square$

Question 1.48. ———————————————————————
Inane ramblings: The argument is valid. There's a moral to this question: Don't assume that it can't be any particular answer until you've examined the math. According to the GRE booklet, 63% of test takers got this question wrong. I assume because they thought

26

(A) was the "sucker's answer" and worked themselves to death trying to find nonexistent errors. □

Question 1.49.

We use the finite case of the *Fundamental theorem of finitely generated abelian groups*.

> Let G be a finite abelian group of order m. Then it is isomorphic to an expression of the form
>
> $$\mathbb{Z}_{k_1} \times \mathbb{Z}_{k_2} \times \ldots \times \mathbb{Z}_{k_n},$$
>
> where k_i divides both k_{i+1} and m for all $i = 1, 2, \ldots, n-1$ and $m = k_1 \cdot k_2 \cdot \ldots \cdot k_n$.

In our situation, we can't have a k_i greater than 4 because that would imply that the characteristic of G would be greater than 4. Thus, the only groups with the property that $x + x + x + x = 0$ are

1. $\mathbb{Z}_4 \times \mathbb{Z}_4$

2. $\mathbb{Z}_2 \times \mathbb{Z}_2 \times \mathbb{Z}_4$

3. $\mathbb{Z}_2 \times \mathbb{Z}_2 \times \mathbb{Z}_2 \times \mathbb{Z}_2$.

□

Question 1.50.

Statement I is a lie. Consider

$$A := \begin{pmatrix} 0 & -1 \\ 1 & 0 \end{pmatrix}.$$

Then

$$A^2 := \begin{pmatrix} -1 & 0 \\ 0 & -1 \end{pmatrix}.$$

Statement II is true, because $\det(A^2) = \det(A) \cdot \det(A) \geq 0$.

Statement III is a fib. What if A has eigenvalues are $\lambda_1 = 1$ and $\lambda_2 = -1$? Doesn't that imply A^2's only eigenvalue would be 1? □

Question 1.51. ————————————————————————

It's not too tough to see

$$\int_0^\infty \lfloor x \rfloor e^{-x} dx = \sum_{n=1}^\infty \int_n^{n+1} n e^{-x} dx.$$

The next few steps are just simple math

$$\sum_{n=1}^\infty \int_n^{n+1} n e^{-x} dx = \sum_{n=1}^\infty -ne^{-n-1} + ne^{-n}$$

$$= \sum_{n=1}^\infty \frac{n(1 - e^{-1})}{e^n}$$

$$= (1 - e^{-1}) \sum_{n=1}^\infty \frac{n}{e^n}$$

$$= (1 - e^{-1}) \sum_{n=1}^\infty n \left(e^{-1}\right)^n.$$

We need to find a formula for

$$\sum_{n=1}^\infty n x^n.$$

A bit of cleverness is required here. But it's only canned cleverness, so you may need to use some of the tricks below for the GRE. First, recall the formula for an infinite geometric series

$$\frac{1}{1 - x} = \sum_{n=0}^\infty x^n,$$

when $|x| < 1$. It follows that

$$\frac{d}{dx}\left(\frac{1}{1 - x}\right) = \frac{1}{(1 - x)^2}$$

$$= \frac{d}{dx}\left(\sum_{n=0}^\infty x^n\right)$$

$$= \sum_{n=1}^\infty n x^{n-1}.$$

28

Multiplying both sides by x yields

$$\frac{x}{(1-x)^2} = \sum_{n=1}^{\infty} nx^n.$$

Notice that the left side of the equation above is what we're looking for, where $x = e^{-1}$. Thus,

$$(1 - e^{-1}) \sum_{n=1}^{\infty} n \left(e^{-1}\right)^n = (1 - e^{-1}) \frac{e^{-1}}{(1 - e^{-1})^2}$$

$$= \frac{1}{e - 1}.$$

$\square$

Question 1.52.

Option (B) is true. Here's why: Recall that $\mathbb{Q}$ is *dense* in $\mathbb{R}$, i.e. $\text{cl}(\mathbb{Q}) = \mathbb{R}$ where cl denotes the closure of a set. It follows that if A is closed $\text{cl}(\mathbb{Q}) = \mathbb{R} \subseteq \text{cl}(A) = A \subseteq \text{cl}(\mathbb{R}) = \mathbb{R}$. Thus $A = \mathbb{R}$.

Let's see why the others are lies. To see why (A) isn't true, consider $A = \mathbb{R} \setminus \{\pi\}$; the set A is open because for each x in A, the open ball centered at x with radius $|x - \pi|/2$ is contained in A. To disprove (C), consider $A := \mathbb{Q} \cup (0, 1)$. The same counterexample disproves (D). Choice (E) is disproved by $A = \mathbb{Q}$, because $\sqrt{2}$ is a limit point. $\square$

Question 1.53.

The minimum value of $f(x, y, z) := x + 4z$ occurs on the boundary of the solid sphere $x^2 + y^2 + z^2 \leq 2$, i.e. the minimum value for f occurs when $x^2 + y^2 + z^2 = 2$.

We need the *method of Lagrange multipliers*:

Suppose $f(x, y, x)$ had first order partial derivatives, and the values x, y, and z satisfy the constraint $g(x, y, z) = k$, where k is a constant. Then

$$f_x(x, y, x) = \lambda g_x(x, y, z), \qquad f_y(x, y, z) = \lambda g_y(x, y, z),$$
$$\text{and} \quad f_z(x, y, z) = \lambda g_z(x, y, z)$$

29

for some λ in $\mathbb{R}$.

Obviously, the function we wish to maximize is $f(x, y, z) := x + 4z$ and our constraint is $g(x, y, z) := x^2 + y^2 + z^2 = 2$. It follows that

$$1 = 2\lambda x, \qquad 0 = 2\lambda y, \quad \text{and} \quad 4 = 2\lambda z.$$

A bit of Algebra shows $y = 0$, and $z = 4x$. Substituting the right sides into the appropriate slots of g yields

$$g(x, 0, 4x) = x^2 + (4x)^2$$
$$= x^2 + 16x^2$$
$$= 17x^2$$
$$= 2.$$

So, $x = \pm\sqrt{2/17} = \pm\sqrt{34}/17$ and $z = \pm 4\sqrt{34}/17$, which means $f(\pm\sqrt{34}/17, 0, \pm 4\sqrt{34}/17) = \pm\sqrt{34}$. Thus, the minimum value of f satisfying $x^2 + y^2 + z^2 = 2$ is $-\sqrt{34}$. $\qquad\square$

Question 1.54. ————————————————————————
Here's a zoomed in version of a shaded circle in figure 1.

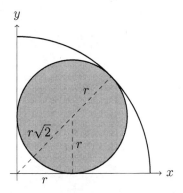

Let's find the ratio of the shaded area in figure 1 to the area of the big circle in figure 1. Suppose the big circle has radius R and the small circle has radius r. Then our picture implies $r + r\sqrt{2} = r(1 + \sqrt{2}) = R$. It follows that $r = R/(1 + \sqrt{2})$. Hence, the ratio of the 4 shaded circles in figure 1 to the area of the big circle is

$$\frac{4\pi \left(\frac{R}{1+\sqrt{2}}\right)^2}{\pi R^2} = \left(\frac{2}{1+\sqrt{2}}\right)^2.$$

Since the ratio of the big circle in figure 1 to the small shaded circles in figure 1 is the same as the ratio of the shaded circles in figure 2 to shaded circles in figure 1, we conclude the answer is $\left(\frac{2}{1+\sqrt{2}}\right)^2$. $\square$

Question 1.55. ───────────────────────────

Zeros are added every time another factor of 10 appears (after perhaps multiplying some numbers together). Since there are more even numbers than multiples of 5, it follows that new zeros are added to the decimal representation of $k!$ whenever k is a multiple of 5.

Let's obtain some rules to help us complete this problem. The number 5! ends in one zero, 10! ends in two zeros, and 15! ends in three. The pattern continues until we reach 25!, which ends in six zeros since 25 has two factors of 5. It's clear this generalizes to the following rule: When k has two factors of 5, two zeros are added to the decimal representation of $k!$. Going from 124! to 125! adds three new zeros, since 125 has three factors of 5. It's clear this generalizes to the following: When k has three factors of 5, three zeros are added to the decimal representation of $k!$. In general: When k has n factors of 5, n new zeros appear in the decimal representation of $k!$.

From here, we consider values of k and use the principles outlined above. Suppose $k = 400$. Then $400! = 400 \cdot 399 \cdot \ldots \cdot 1$ has 80 numbers which have 5 as a factor, 16 of which are multiples of 25, and 3 are multiples of 125. It follows that 400! will have $80 + 16 + 3 = 99$ zeros. Clearly 401!, 402!, 403!, and 404! will also have 99 zeros, since $401, 402, 403,$ and 404 have no new factors of five. $\square$

Question 1.56. ───────────────────────────

For those unfamiliar with the definition of a *metric*, see the glossary at the end of this booklet.

Since $r^2 < |r|$ when $|r| < 1$, ω fails the triangle inequality. For example, say $x = 1, y = 0$, and $z = 1/2$. Then $\omega(1,0) = 1$ and $\omega(1, 1/2) + \omega(1/2, 0) = 1/4 + 1/4 = 1/2$.

This is where we would move on during the test, but let's make a few more remarks. Verifying that (A)–(C) are metrics doesn't add much insight. Instead, we'll explain why we would want to examine τ and ω first during the GRE:

(A) It looks like δ behaves like the discrete metric.

(B) It looks like ρ behaves like the Euclidian metric for values "close" together, and behaves like the discrete metric elsewhere.

(C) It looks like σ is equivalent to the Euclidian metric.

Now let's verify that τ is a metric. We know $d(x, y) = |x - y|$ is a metric, and non-negativity and symmetry of τ follow directly from this. Next, note that

$$f(x) := \frac{x}{1 + x}$$

is monotonically increasing for all non-negative numbers. You can prove this, for example, by taking the derivative. Hence, τ passes the triangle inequality criterion, because

$$
\begin{aligned}
\tau(x, y) &= f\left(|x - y|\right) \\
&\leq f\left(|x - z| + |z - y|\right) \\
&= \frac{|x - z| + |z - y|}{1 + |x - z| + |z - y|} \\
&= \frac{|x - z|}{1 + |x - z| + |z - y|} + \frac{|z - y|}{1 + |x - z| + |z - y|} \\
&\leq \frac{|x - z|}{1 + |x - z|} + \frac{|z - y|}{1 + |z - y|} \\
&= \tau(x, z) + \tau(z, y),
\end{aligned}
$$

for all z. $\qquad\square$

Question 1.57. ⎯⎯⎯⎯⎯⎯⎯⎯⎯⎯⎯⎯⎯⎯⎯⎯⎯⎯⎯⎯⎯⎯

It's clear that the answer is (E), since n^n grows far more rapidly than $n!$, and $0 \leq \frac{x^{2n}}{1 + x^{2n}} < 1$ for all x. But let's work this out in case it's not clear to you.

From the remarks above, we know

$$0 \le \frac{n! x^{2n}}{n^n \left(1 + x^{2n}\right)} \le \frac{n!}{n^n},$$

for $n = 1, 2, 3, \ldots$. So convergence of $\sum \frac{n!}{n^n}$ implies convergence of $\sum \frac{n! x^{2n}}{n^n (1 + x^{2n})}$.

We will use the *ratio test* to prove $\sum \frac{n!}{n^n}$ converges.

$$
\begin{aligned}
\lim_{n \to \infty} \left| \frac{\frac{(n+1)!}{(n+1)^{n+1}}}{\frac{n!}{n^n}} \right| &= \lim_{n \to \infty} \frac{(n+1)!}{(n+1)^{n+1}} \frac{n^n}{n!} \\
&= \lim_{n \to \infty} \frac{(n+1)}{(n+1)^{n+1}} \frac{n^n}{1} \\
&= \lim_{n \to \infty} \left(\frac{n}{n+1} \right)^n \\
&= \frac{1}{e} \\
&< 1
\end{aligned}
$$

Before we move on to the next problem, let's see why $\lim_{t \to \infty} \left(\frac{t}{t+1} \right)^t = 1/e$. Let $y = \left(\frac{t}{t+1} \right)^t$. Then, taking the natural log of both sides and using the power rule for logarithms on the right side of the equation yields, $\log y = t \log \frac{t}{t+1}$. It follows that

$$
\begin{aligned}
\lim_{t \to \infty} \log y &= \lim_{t \to \infty} t \log \frac{t}{t+1} \\
&= \lim_{t \to \infty} \frac{\log \left(\frac{t}{t+1} \right)}{\frac{1}{t}} \\
&\overset{LH}{=} \lim_{t \to \infty} \frac{\frac{t+1}{t} \cdot \frac{1}{(t+1)^2}}{-\frac{1}{t^2}} \\
&= \lim_{t \to \infty} \frac{-t^2}{t^2 + t} \\
&= \lim_{t \to \infty} \frac{-1}{1 + \frac{1}{t}} \\
&= -1.
\end{aligned}
$$

33

And $\lim_{t\to\infty} \log y = -1$ implies $\lim_{t\to\infty} y = 1/e$. Note "LH" in the string of equations above is short for *L'Hôpital's rule*. A list of *logarithm properties* is located in the glossary. $\square$

Question 1.58.

Let's introduce some notation. Since A and B are similar, let's say $PAP^{-1} = B$. Also let $\text{tr}(C)$ denote the trace of C.

Onto our problem. Property I is true. Suppose $PAP^{-1} = B$. Then

$$P(A - 2I)P^{-1} = PAP^{-1} - 2PIP^{-1}$$
$$= PAP^{-1} - 2I$$
$$= B - 2I.$$

Property II is valid: Recall $\text{tr}(AB) = \text{tr}(BA)$. In our case

$$\text{tr}(B) = \text{tr}\left(P(AP^{-1})\right)$$
$$= \text{tr}\left((AP^{-1})P\right)$$
$$= \text{tr}(AI)$$
$$= \text{tr}(A).$$

Property III holds too: If $PAP^{-1} = B$, then

$$B^{-1} = (PAP^{-1})^{-1}$$
$$= (P^{-1})^{-1}(PA)^{-1}$$
$$= PA^{-1}P^{-1}.$$

$\square$

Question 1.59.

Recall the *necessary and sufficient condition for a function to be analytic*:

The function $f(z) = u(x, y) + iv(x, y)$ is analytic if and only if $u_x(x, y) = v_y(x, y)$ and $u_y(x, y) = -v_x(x, y)$.

Hence, if f is analytic, then $g_y(x,y) = \frac{\partial}{\partial x}(2x+3y) = 2$ and $g_x(x,y) = -\frac{\partial}{\partial y}(2x+3y) = -3$. It follows that $g(x,y) = 2y+h_1(x)$ and $g(x,y) = -3x + h_2(y)$. In conjunction, these two expressions imply $g(x,y) = -3x + 2y + C$, where C is a constant. We know $g(2,3) = -3(2) + 2(3) + C = C = 1$. Thus, $g(7,3) = -3(7) + 2(3) + 1 = -15 + 1 = -14$. □

Question 1.60. ———————————————————————

The Dihedral group of order 10 is, by definition, the group of symmetries of a pentagon. There's no reason to believe the symmetries of a pentagram are any different. □

Question 1.61. ———————————————————————

A list of definitions for *cardinal arithmetic* is contained in the glossary. Also, recall the *Schröder-Berstein theorem*, which states:

If $|A| \leq |B|$ and $|B| \leq |A|$, then $|A| = |B|$.

Onto our problem.

(A) Recall $|\mathbb{R}| = 2^{\aleph_0}$.

(B) $\left|\{f \mid f : \mathbb{Z} \to \mathbb{Z}\}\right| = \aleph_0^{\aleph_0}$, and $2^{\aleph_0} \leq \aleph_0^{\aleph_0} \leq \left(2^{\aleph_0}\right)^{\aleph_0} = 2^{\aleph_0 \cdot \aleph_0} = 2^{\aleph_0}$. Thus, by the Schröder-Berstein theorem, we conclude $\left|\{f \mid f : \mathbb{Z} \to \mathbb{Z}\}\right| = 2^{\aleph_0}$. Note $|\mathbb{Z}| = \aleph_0$.

(C) It's clear $\left|\{f \mid f : \mathbb{R} \to \{0,1\}\}\right| = 2^{2^{\aleph_0}}$.

(D) Let $\mathcal{F}$ denote the set of finite subsets of $\mathbb{R}$. Because $f : \mathbb{R} \to \mathcal{F}$ defined by $f : x \mapsto \{x\}$ is one-to-one, it's clear $2^{\aleph_0} \leq |\mathcal{F}|$. Let

$\mathcal{F}_n$ denotes the set of subsets of $\mathbb{R}$ with n elements. Then

$$|\mathcal{F}| = \sum_{n=0}^{\infty} |\mathcal{F}_n|$$

$$\leq \sum_{n=1}^{\infty} 2^{\aleph_0}$$

$$= \aleph_0 \cdot 2^{\aleph_0}$$

$$= 2^{\aleph_0}.$$

So, by the Schröder-Berstein theorem, $|\mathcal{F}| = 2^{\aleph_0}$.

(E) It's clear the set of polynomials has the same cardinality as $\mathcal{F}$.

Since $2^{2^{\aleph_0}}$ is different than the others, the correct answer must be (C). □

Question 1.62.

Property I must be true. The argument goes as follows. The continuous image of a compact space is compact. Thus, for f continuous and real valued, $f(K) \subseteq \mathbb{R}$ must be compact. By the *Heine-Borel theorem*, $f(K)$ must be closed and bounded.

Property II is also true. We'll prove it using the other direction of the Heine–Borel theorem. If K where unbounded, then the real valued function $f(x) := \|x\|$ would be unbounded, where $\|\cdot\|$ denotes the Euclidian metric. If K weren't closed, then it wouldn't contain one of its limit points, say k. Then $f(x) := 1/\|x - k\|$ would be an unbounded continuous function. Thus, since K is a closed and bounded subset of $\mathbb{R}^n$, it must be compact.

Property III is a lie. Consider $[0, 1] \cup [2, 3]$; clearly that's a compact set and it's not connected. □

Question 1.63.

The graph of f is horizontal when $f'(x) = 0$. Obviously, this means we need to find the derivative. For $x \neq 0$, $f(x) = xe^{-x^2 - x^{-2}}$, therefore

$$f'(x) = e^{-x^2 - x^{-2}} + x(-2x + 2x^{-3})e^{-x^2 - x^{-2}}$$
$$= e^{-x^2 - x^{-2}}\left(1 - 2x^2 + 2x^{-2}\right)$$
$$= \frac{-2x^4 + x^2 + 2}{x^2}e^{-x^2 - x^{-2}}$$

for $x \neq 0$. It's easy to see $f'(x) = 0$ occurs when $-2x^4 + x^2 + 2 = 0$ which implies $x^2 = \frac{-1 \pm \sqrt{17}}{-4} = \frac{1 \pm \sqrt{17}}{4}$. Since $x^2 \geq 0$ we exclude $\frac{1 - \sqrt{17}}{4}$ as a possibility. So we've found 2 values of x that do the job so far. Namely,

$$x = \pm\frac{\sqrt{1 + \sqrt{17}}}{2}.$$

The only other time, possibly, when $f'(x) = 0$ is at $x = 0$. For this case, we need to go back to the derivative definition. We have

$$f'(0) = \lim_{h \to 0} \frac{f(h) - f(0)}{h}$$
$$= \lim_{h \to 0} \frac{he^{-h^2 - h^{-2}}}{h}$$
$$= \lim_{h \to 0} e^{-h^2 - h^{-2}}$$
$$= 0.$$

Note $-h^2 - h^{-2} \to -\infty$ as $h \to 0$. Thus, there are a total of three values of x that make f parallel to the x-axis. $\qquad\square$

Question 1.64. ————————————————————————————
First, it's clear that

$$f(x) = \lim_{n \to \infty} \frac{x^n}{1 + x^n} = \begin{cases} 1/2, & x = 1 \\ 0, & x \neq 1 \end{cases}$$

As such, we can conclude that $\{f_n\}$ converges point-wise, so I is true. However, $\{f_n\}$ does not converge uniformly to f by the contrapositive of the *uniform convergence theorem*, which disproves II. Here's the uniform convergence theorem (from Wikipedia):

Suppose $\{f_n\}$ is a sequence of continuous functions that converge point-wise to the function f. If $\{f_n\}$ converges uniformly to f on an interval S, then f is continuous on S.

It's clear that III is true. One way to make this conclusion is by considering the fact that the set of discontinuities of f has measure 0. To give a more intuitive argument for III, the area under the graph of $f_n(x)$ goes to zero as n goes to infinity, so $\int_0^1 f_n(x)\,dx \to 0$ as $n \to \infty$. Clearly, $\int_0^1 f(x)\,dx = 0$, since there's no area under a point. $\square$

Question 1.65. ————————————————
Statement I is true. Consider $f(x) := |\sin(2\pi x)|$; $f(1/2) = 0$, $f(1/4) = 1$, and every value between follows from the intermediate value theorem.

Statement II is false. The image of a compact set under a continuous map is compact. It follows that $f([0,1])$ must be compact when f is continuous. But the *Heine-Borel theorem* implies $f([0,1])$ must be closed and $(0,1)$ is open. Thus $f([0,1]) \neq (0,1)$, if f is continuous.

Statement III is also false. Suppose for the sake of contradiction that $g : (0,1) \to [0,1]$ is one-to-one and onto. If g is one-to-one, then it must be monotonic. Since g is onto there exists an x_1 in $(0,1)$ such that $g(x_1) = 1$. But this means g must be increasing for values of x less than x_1 and decreasing for values greater than x_1. This contradicts monotonicity. $\square$

Question 1.66. ————————————————
Statement I is false. Consider the quaternions. Since every nonzero element has an inverse, there are no proper ideals. Furthermore, 1 is an element of the quaternion. So all the criteria listed in the question are satisfied. But $ij = k$ and $ji = -k$.

Statement II is true. Let x be an arbitrary element in $R \setminus \{0\}$. We will prove x has an inverse. Consider $xR := \{xr : r \in R\}$. We want to prove that xR is a right ideal. Let's first verify that xR is a subgroup.

Closed under addition: Suppose xr and xs are in xR.

38

Then $xr + xs = x(r + s)$ is in xR.

Contains the additive identity: This is clear, since $x0 = 0$.

Contains additive inverses: It's clear $x(-r)$ is in xR, and $x(-r) + xr = xr + x(-r) = x(r - r) = x0 = 0$.

The subgroup xR is a right ideal, because s in R implies rs is in R, which implies $(xr)s = x(rs)$ is in xR. It follow that $xR = R$. This is because $x = x1$ is in xR and the only right ideals are $\{0\}$ and R. Hence, there is x' in R such that $xx' = 1$, so every element must have a right inverse because $x \neq 0$ was arbitrary. The element x' is also a left inverses. This is because $(x'x)(x'x) = x'(xx')x = x'x$ and multiplying both sides by the right inverse of $x'x$ proves $x'x = 1$. Thus every nonzero element has an inverse and we conclude that R is a division ring.

Statement III is false. Consider $\mathbb{Z}_3$. It's a ring, and $\mathbb{Z}_3$ only has trivial ideals, since it's a field. □

Chapter 2

GRE mathematics subject test GR9768 solutions

Question 2.1. ───────────────────────────────

Using the *Fundamental theorem of Calculus*, it follows that $F'(x) = \log x$, since the lower limit is a constant. □

Question 2.2. ───────────────────────────────

Let's look at a few iterations:

$$F(2) = 2 + \frac{1}{2}, \quad F(3) = 2 + \frac{1}{2} + \frac{1}{2} \quad F(4) = 2 + \frac{1}{2}(2) + \frac{1}{2}$$
$$= 2 + \frac{1}{2}(2), \qquad = 2 + \frac{1}{2}(3).$$

From here, it's not too tough to see

$$F(n) = 2 + \frac{1}{2}(n-1).$$

Therefore,

$$F(101) = 2 + \frac{1}{2}(101 - 1) = 52.$$

□

Question 2.3. ——————————————————————

The standard practice for finding the inverse of a matrix M is to put the matrix $(M|I)$ into reduced row-echelon form, where I is the $n \times n$ identity matrix. After this has been completed the right side of the augment matrix will be M^{-1}. However, the formula for the *inverse of a* 2×2 *invertible matrix*

$$A := \begin{pmatrix} a & b \\ c & d \end{pmatrix} \quad \text{is} \quad A^{-1} = \begin{pmatrix} d & -b \\ -c & a \end{pmatrix}.$$

This immediately gives us

$$\begin{pmatrix} a & -b \\ b & a \end{pmatrix}^{-1} = \frac{1}{a^2 + b^2} \begin{pmatrix} a & b \\ -b & a \end{pmatrix}.$$

$\square$

Question 2.4. ——————————————————————

The first step is to find b. To do this, we compute the two integrals:

$$\int_0^b x \, dx = \frac{x^2}{2} \Big|_0^b \qquad \text{and} \qquad \int_0^b x^2 \, dx = \frac{x^3}{3} \Big|_0^b$$

$$= \frac{b^2}{2} \qquad\qquad\qquad\qquad = \frac{b^3}{3}.$$

It follows that $b^2/2 = b^3/3$. Since $b \neq 0$, we conclude $b = 3/2$.

To find the place where our two graphs intersect, we let $x^2 = x$. It follows that $x = 0$ or $x = 1$; the latter of which is the desired result. Hence, $1 \leq x \leq 3/2$ in the shaded region.

All that is left is to use integration to compute our area. Since $y = x^2$ is above $y = x$, the solution is

$$\int_1^{3/2} x^2 - x \, dx = \frac{x^3}{3} - \frac{x^2}{2} \Big|_1^{3/2}$$

$$= \frac{1}{6}.$$

42

Question 2.5.

Using the *first derivative test*, it's clear that f has a relative minimum at $x \approx -3$, a relative maximum at $x \approx 6$, and a relative minimum at $x \approx 10$. This is already enough to conclude that the solution is (E). □

Question 2.6.

Let's take a look at the first few p's:

$$p = 0 \quad \text{when} \quad i = 1$$
$$p = 1 \quad \text{when} \quad i = 2$$
$$p = 2 \quad \text{when} \quad i = 4$$
$$\vdots$$
$$p = n \quad \text{when} \quad i = 2^n.$$

From here, we simply note the first $i = 2^n \geq 999$ occurs when $n = 10$. Thus the p that will be printed is $p = 10$. □

Question 2.7.

Note that one of the *Pythagorean identities* is $\sin^2 x + \cos^2 x = 1$. Hence, the set $\{(\sin t, \cos t) : -\pi/2 \leq t \leq 0\}$ is part of a circle of radius 1. From the unit-circle in precalculus we know $-1 \leq \sin t \leq 0$ and $0 \leq \cos t \leq 1$, when $-\pi/2 \leq t \leq 0$, so the graph is in the second quadrant. The only option that satisfies these criteria is (B). □

Question 2.8.

This is a simple *u*-substitution. Let $u = 1 + x^2$ which implies $du = 2x \ dx$.

Hence,

$$\int_0^1 \frac{x}{1+x^2}\, dx = \frac{1}{2}\int_0^1 \frac{2x}{1+x^2}\, dx$$

$$= \frac{1}{2}\int_{x=0}^1 \frac{du}{u}$$

$$= \frac{1}{2}\int_{u=1}^2 \frac{du}{u}$$

$$= \frac{1}{2}\log|u|\Big|_1^2$$

$$= \frac{1}{2}(\log|2| - \log|1|)$$

$$= \frac{1}{2}\log 2$$

$$= \log\sqrt{2}.$$

Lists of *antiderivatives* and *logarithm properties* are in the glossary. □

Question 2.9.

The number of one-to-one functions $f : S \to S$ is simply the number of permutations of the list $(1,\ 2,\ 3, \ldots, k)$, which is $k!$. □

Question 2.10.

The function g is continuous at a if and only if

$$\lim_{x \to a} g(x) = g(a),$$

or equivalently if and only if

$$\lim_{n \to \infty} g(a_n) = g(a)$$

for every sequence $\{a_n\}_n$ such that $a_n \to a$ as $n \to \infty$.

Let $\{q_n\}_n$ be a rational sequence such that $q_n \to a$ and let $\{y_n\}_n$ be an irrational sequence such that $y_n \to a$ as $n \to \infty$. Then

$$\lim_{n \to \infty} g(q_n) = 1 \quad \text{and} \quad \lim_{n \to \infty} g(y_n) = e^a.$$

44

Thus g is only continuous at a when $e^a = 1$. Using *logarithm properties*, it follows that $a = 0$. □

Question 2.11. ────────────────────────────────

Suppose $x \geq y$, which implies $x - y \geq 0$. The absolute value does nothing to non-negative values so $|x - y| = x - y$. It follows that

$$\frac{x + y + |x - y|}{2} = \frac{x + y + x - y}{2}$$

$$= x.$$

Since $|x - y| = |-(y - x)| = |y - x|$, an almost identical argument shows

$$\frac{x + y + |x - y|}{2} = y,$$

when $y > x$.

We conclude that $(x + y + |x - y|)/2$ is the maximum of x and y. □

Question 2.12. ────────────────────────────────

Let's go through the options that are false first. Choice (A) is false. Consider $B := [0, 1)$; B isn't open but it doesn't contain its *least upper bound* of 1. Choice (B) is disproved by $B := (0, 1)$; B is open and doesn't contain its least upper bound of 1. Choice (D) is debunked by $B := (0, 1)$ and the sequence $\{1 - 1/(n+1)\}_n$. Choice (E) is an untruth too. Consider $B = (0, 1)$; 1 is the least upper bound of B, but every open ball containing 1 contains values of B.

Thus by the process of elimination we select (C). However, we're not being timed, so let's prove it! Suppose b is not a limit point of B. Then there is some $r > 0$ such that the open ball, with center b and radius r, contains no points of B. It's clear that $b - r/2$ is in our ball, but it is less than b and still greater than every value in B. This is a contradiction of the definition of a least upper bound. It follows that every open ball with center b has points in B. So b is a limit point. □

Question 2.13. ————————————————————
We know from the *probability properties* in precalculus that for events A and B in the sample space

$$P(A \cup B) = P(A) + P(B) - P(A \cap B),$$

or with C also an event in the sample space

$$P(A \cup B \cup C) = P(A) + P(B \cup C) - P(A \cap (B \cup C))$$
$$= P(A) + P(B) + P(C) - P(B \cap C) - \Big(P(A \cap B)$$
$$+ P(A \cap C) - P(A \cap B \cap C)\Big)$$
$$= P(A) + P(B) + P(C) - P(A \cap B) - P(A \cap C)$$
$$- P(B \cap C) + P(A \cap B \cap C).$$

In our case, getting two blue, two red, or two yellow socks is mutually exclusive, so $P(A \cap B) = P(A \cap C) = P(B \cap C) = P(A \cap B \cap C) = 0$.

All that is left is to compute the probabilities of getting 2 red, 2 blue, and 2 yellow socks, and to add everything together. The probability of picking two blue socks is

$$\frac{2}{8} \cdot \frac{1}{7} = \frac{1}{28},$$

two red's is

$$\frac{4}{8} \cdot \frac{3}{7} = \frac{6}{28},$$

and two yellow's is

$$\frac{2}{8} \cdot \frac{1}{7} = \frac{1}{28}.$$

Therefore the probability of picking two socks of identical color is

$$\frac{1}{28} + \frac{6}{28} + \frac{1}{28} = \frac{2}{7}.$$

□

Question 2.14. ───────────────────────────

In general, the negation of "For each A there exists B such that C " is

"There exists A such that for each B not C."

This can be proven with a truth-table. Furthermore, the negation of "If D, then E" is

"D and not E."

Thus, the negation of "For each s in $\mathbb{R}$, there exists an r in $\mathbb{R}$ such that if $f(r) > 0$, then $g(s) > 0$" must be

"There exists s in $\mathbb{R}$ such that for each r in $\mathbb{R}$ $f(r) > 0$ and $g(s) \not> 0$."

Since $\not>$ is the the same as $>$, we conclude that the answer is (C). □

Question 2.15. ───────────────────────────

Let's go through the ones that are false first. Choice (A) is wrong. Since $a < g(x) < x < b$ for all x in (a, b), $|g(x)| < \max\{|a|, |b|\}$ for all x in (a, b). Choice (C) is an untruth. Consider $g(x) := -\sqrt{|x|}$ on the interval $(-1, 0)$. Choice (D) and (E) are debunked by $g(x) = x - x^2$ on $(0,1)$. See the graph below.

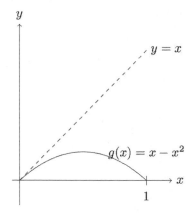

We have already provided enough information to conclude (B) is correct, but let's prove since the clock isn't ticking down. Suppose

$g(x) = k$, where k is a constant. By the stated hypotheses, $a < g(x) = k < x < b$. Therefore $(a + k)/2$ is in (a, b). However,

$$g\left(\frac{a+k}{2}\right) = k \not< \frac{a+k}{2},$$

which contradicts the criteria required for g. $\qquad\qquad\square$

Question 2.16. ⎯⎯⎯⎯⎯⎯⎯⎯⎯⎯⎯⎯⎯⎯⎯⎯⎯⎯⎯⎯⎯⎯⎯⎯⎯
If $(1, 2, m, 5)$ is a linear combination of $(0, 1, 1, 1)$, $(0, 0, 0, 1)$, and $(1, 1, 2, 0)$ then there exists c_1, c_2, and c_3 such that $(1, 2, m, 5) = c_1(0, 1, 1, 1) + c_2(0, 0, 0, 1) + c_3(1, 1, 2, 0)$. Rewriting our row vectors as column vectors, and placing them in a matrix gives us

$$\begin{pmatrix} 0 & 0 & 1 \\ 1 & 0 & 1 \\ 1 & 0 & 2 \\ 1 & 1 & 0 \end{pmatrix} \begin{pmatrix} c_1 \\ c_2 \\ c_3 \end{pmatrix} = \begin{pmatrix} 1 \\ 2 \\ m \\ 5 \end{pmatrix}.$$

As an augmented matrix, our equation becomes

$$\left(\begin{array}{ccc|c} 0 & 0 & 1 & 1 \\ 1 & 0 & 1 & 2 \\ 1 & 0 & 2 & m \\ 1 & 1 & 0 & 5 \end{array} \right).$$

Row reducing yields

$$\left(\begin{array}{ccc|c} 1 & 0 & 1 & 2 \\ 0 & 1 & -1 & 3 \\ 0 & 0 & 1 & m-2 \\ 0 & 0 & 0 & 3-m \end{array} \right).$$

Thus, $m = 3$. All other m's would lead to the contradiction $0 = 3 - m$. $\qquad\qquad\square$

Question 2.17. ────────────────────────────────

A little algebra shows $f(x + 1) = f(x) + \Delta f(x)$ and $\Delta f(x + 1) = \Delta f(x) + \Delta^2 f(x)$. Hence,

$$f(2) = f(1) + \Delta f(1) \qquad\qquad f(3) = f(2) + \Delta f(2)$$
$$= -1 + 4 \qquad\qquad\qquad\qquad\quad = 3 - 2$$
$$= 3, \qquad\qquad\qquad\qquad\qquad\quad = 1,$$

and

$$f(4) = f(3) + \Delta f(3)$$
$$= 1 + \Delta f(2) + \Delta^2 f(2)$$
$$= 1 - 2 + 6$$
$$= 5.$$

$\square$

Question 2.18. ────────────────────────────────

It's clear $A(r) = \pi(1 - r^2)$ and $a(r) = \pi(1 - r)^2$. Thus,

$$\lim_{r \to 1^-} \frac{A(r)}{a(r)} = \lim_{r \to 1^-} \frac{\pi(1 - r^2)}{\pi(1 - r)^2}$$
$$= \lim_{r \to 1^-} \frac{1 + r}{1 - r}$$
$$= \infty.$$

$\square$

Question 2.19. ────────────────────────────────

Cayley table I is a *group*. It's clear I is closed under our binary operation and a is the identity element. Careful examination shows that I is generated by b: $b^2 = c$, $b^3 = d$, and $b^4 = a$. So every element has an inverse; b^m has an inverse of b^{4-m} for all m. Associativity holds trivially.

Cayley table II is not a group, because $(d \cdot c) \cdot c = c$ and $d \cdot (c \cdot c) = d$. To make a quick tip for test takers: Checking associativity case by case takes too long. Instead, notice a is listed twice in row c. This is impossible because it means c has two inverses which never happens in groups, so the Cayley table must fail some axiom. Stopping there seems to be consistent with best test taking practices.

Lastly, Cayley table III is not a group. It's clear a is the identity element for III. However, there is no a in row c, which means c has no inverse. $\square$

Question 2.20.

Let's go through each option. Property I is true, because

$$\lim_{x \to 0} \frac{f(x)}{x} = \lim_{x \to 0} \frac{f(0+x) - 0}{x}$$
$$= \lim_{x \to 0} \frac{f(0+x) - f(0)}{x},$$

which is precisely the definition of the derivative. Property II is false. Consider $f(x) = \sin x$;

$$\lim_{x \to 0} \frac{\sin x}{x} \overset{LH}{=} \lim_{x \to 0} \frac{\cos x}{1}$$
$$= 1.$$

Note LH denotes the use of L'Hôspital's rule. Property III must be true, because

$$\lim_{x \to 0} f(x) = \lim_{x \to 0} x \cdot \frac{f(x)}{x}$$
$$= 0 \cdot L$$
$$= 0.$$

$\square$

Question 2.21. ───────────────────────────────────

We need to find the equation of the tangent line. The point of tangency is $(0,1)$. We need the slope of $y = \frac{1}{8}x^2 + \frac{1}{2}x + 1$ at $(0,1)$. It's clear $y'(x) = \frac{1}{4}x + \frac{1}{2}$. Hence $y'(0) = 1/2$. Therefore our tangent line is $y = \frac{1}{2}x + 1$, which gives us the following graph.

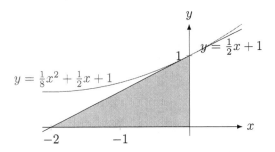

Thus, the region is simply a triangle and it has area $\frac{1}{2}(2)(1) = 1$. $\qquad\square$

Question 2.22. ───────────────────────────────────

The set of non-negative integers is not a *group* because it does not have additive inverses. For example, the additive inverse of 1, i.e. -1, is not in $\{n \in \mathbb{Z} : n \geq 0\}$. Hence, the set of non-negative integers is not a subgroup either, because a subgroup of $\mathbb{Z}$ is a group contained within $\mathbb{Z}$. $\qquad\square$

Question 2.23. ────────────────────────────

Consider the diagram shown below, and in particular $\triangle BAO$.

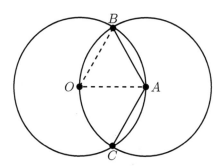

It's clear $BO = AB = AO$. Since the lengths of the sides are the same, it must be the case that angle $AOB \cong$ angle $ABO \cong$ angle OAB. It follows that each angle must have measure of 60°. By symmetry, the measure of angle $OAC = 60°$. Therefore the measure of angle $BAC = 120°$. □

Question 2.24. ────────────────────────────

Suppose $x := (x_1, x_2, x_3, x_4)$ is orthogonal to both $(0, 1, 1, 1)$ and $(1, 1, 1, 0)$. Because the dot product of two orthogonal vectors is 0,

$$x \cdot (0, 1, 1, 1) = x_2 + x_3 + x_4 = 0$$

and

$$x \cdot (1, 1, 1, 0) = x_1 + x_2 + x_3 = 0.$$

A bit of arithmetic shows

$$x_1 = x_4, \quad x_2 = -x_3 - x_4,$$

and both x_3 and x_4 are free. Hence, any vector of the form

$$\begin{aligned} x &= (-x_4, -x_3 - x_4, x_3, x_4) \\ &= (0, -x_3, x_3, 0) + (-x_4, -x_4, 0, x_4) \\ &= x_3(0, -1, 1, 0) + x_4(1, -1, 0, 1) \end{aligned}$$

will be orthogonal to our two vectors. So a *basis* is $\{(0, -1, 1, 0), (1, -1, 0, 1)\}$. Since all finite bases for a vector space have the same number of elements, our basis must have two elements too, which narrows our choices down to (B) and (C). It cannot be (B) because $(1, 1, 1, 0) \cdot (0, 1, 1, 1) \neq 0$.

Another approach is as follows. (1) Examine what choices are consistent with a basis, leaving (A), (B), and (C). (2) Check the orthogonality between the potential bases' elements and our vectors one-by-one, leaving (A) and (C). And (3) of the remaining choices pick the set with the largest cardinality, specifically (C). This process takes more or less the same amount of time as the solution described above, but checking linear independence is often time consuming when dealing with more than two vectors. □

Question 2.25. —————————————————
According to the *extreme value theorem*, f has an absolute maximum because f is real-valued and its domain is *compact*. The maximum will be on the boundary or at a relative maximum. From Calculus, we know that relative extrema occur when the partial derivatives are undefined or zero. But $f_x(x, y) = 5$ and $f_y(x, y) = -4$, so f has no relative extrema. Hence, the maximum of f must be on the boundary.

Let's graph the domain of f.

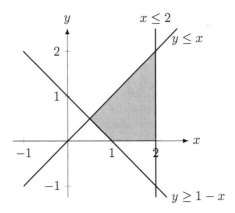

Suppose $y = x$. Then $f(x, x) = x$ and $1/2 \leq x \leq 2$. Therefore

$f(2, 2) = 2$ is the maximum value of f on $y = x$.

Assume $y = 1 - x$. Then $f(x, 1 - x) = 5x - 4(1 - x) = 9x - 4$ and $1/2 \leq x \leq 1$. Therefore $f(1, 0) = 5$ is the maximum value of f on $y = 1 - x$.

Say $y = 0$. Then $f(x, 0) = 5x$ and $1 \leq x \leq 2$. Therefore $f(2, 0) = 10$ is the maximum on $y = 0$.

The last boundary is $x = 2$, which implies $f(2, y) = 10 - 4y$ and $0 \leq y \leq 2$. It's clear that the $y = 0$ maximizes f on this boundary and $f(2, 0) = 10$.

We conclude that the absolute maximum value of f on the domain specified is 10. $\qquad\square$

Question 2.26.

Extrapolating from the *extreme value theorem*, it's clear that absolute extrema occur at relative extrema or else

$$\lim_{x \to -\infty} f(x) \quad \text{and} \quad \lim_{x \to -\infty} f(x)$$

will be values greater or smaller than f at our relative extrema. Let's compute the pieces.

We have

$$\lim_{x \to \infty} f(x) = \lim_{x \to \infty} -x^2 + 2$$

$$= -\infty$$

and

$$\lim_{x \to \infty} f(x) = \lim_{x \to -\infty} -x^2 + 4x - 2$$

$$= -\infty.$$

We need the derivative of f, so we can find our critical numbers. It's not too hard to see

$$f'(x) = \begin{cases} -2x + 4 & \text{if } x < 1, \\ -2x & \text{if } x > 1. \end{cases}$$

Note in particular that $x = 1$ is a critical number since $f'(1)$ is undefined because

$$\lim_{x \to 1^-} f'(x) = 2 \quad \text{and} \quad \lim_{x \to 1^+} f'(x) = -2.$$

This is because *derivatives have no "simple discontinuities"*, i.e. the left and right limits of a derivative agree if both exist. It's clear f' has no other critical numbers, because $-2x + 4$ is never zero when $x < 1$ and $-2x$ is never zero when $x > 1$.

It follows that there $f(1) = 1$ is our absolute maximum, since it is the only relative extreme and f decreases without bounds as $x \to \infty$ and $x \to -\infty$. $\square$

Question 2.27.
This is tricky if you overthink it. However, obtaining the answer is quite trivial. If $f(x) = f(1 - x)$ for all x, then

$$\frac{d}{dx} f(x) = \frac{d}{dx} f(1 - x).$$

Hence,

$$f'(x) = -f'(1 - x).$$

Evaluating at $x = 0$ shows

$$f'(0) = -f'(1).$$

$\square$

Question 2.28.
This reduces to an equivalent problem with *bases*, since every subspace has a basis. Let $\mathcal{B}$ be a basis for V, and $\mathcal{B}_1 \subseteq \mathcal{B}$ and $\mathcal{B}_2 \subseteq \mathcal{B}$ be bases for V_1 and V_2 respectively. If we assume the basis of $V_1 \cap V_2$ is as small as possible, then $\mathcal{B}_1 \cup \mathcal{B}_2 = \mathcal{B}$. The *inclusion-exclusion principle* implies

$$|\mathcal{B}| = |\mathcal{B}_1 \cup \mathcal{B}_2|$$
$$= |\mathcal{B}_1| + |\mathcal{B}_2| - |\mathcal{B}_1 \cap \mathcal{B}_2|$$
$$= 12 - |\mathcal{B}_1 \cap \mathcal{B}_2|.$$

Since $|\mathcal{B}| = 10$, we have

$$12 - |\mathcal{B}_1 \cap \mathcal{B}_2| = 10.$$

It follows that

$$|\mathcal{B}_1 \cap \mathcal{B}_2| = 2.$$

$\square$

Question 2.29.

We will use *integration by parts*. Let $u = x$ and $dv = p''(x)\,dx$. Then $du = dx$ and $v = p'(x)$. Therefore

$$\int_0^2 xp''(x)\,dx = xp'(x) - \int p'(x)\,dx \Big|_0^2$$

$$= xp'(x) - p(x) \Big|_0^2$$

$$= 2p'(2) - p(2) + p(0)$$

$$= 2(-1) - 4 + 4$$

$$= -2.$$

$\square$

Question 2.30.

Choice (A) is false. Suppose $\mathbf{0}$ is in $\mathcal{B}$. Since the dimension of V is greater than 1, there is another vector $\mathbf{v} \neq \mathbf{0}$ in $\mathcal{B}$. But $0\mathbf{v} = \mathbf{0}$, which contradicts the fact that the elements of a *basis* are linearly independent.

Choice (B) is a lie. Suppose the elements of $\mathcal{A}$ span V and $\mathcal{A} \subset \mathcal{B}$. Choose $\mathbf{v}$ in $\mathcal{B} \setminus \mathcal{A}$. Because $\mathcal{B} \subset V$,

$$\mathbf{v} = c_1\mathbf{v}_1 + c_2\mathbf{v}_2 + \ldots + c_n\mathbf{v}_n$$

for some $\mathbf{v}_i$ in $\mathcal{A}$ and c_i in $\mathbb{F}$. This contradicts linear independence of $\mathcal{B}$.

Choice (C) is impossible. Suppose $\mathcal{B} \subset \mathcal{C}$, where $\mathcal{C}$ is a linearly independent subset of V. Choose $\mathbf{v}$ in $\mathcal{C} \setminus \mathcal{B}$. Since $\mathcal{B}$ is a basis of V, there exist $c_1, c_2, \ldots c_n$ in $\mathbb{F}$ and $\mathbf{v}_1, \mathbf{v}_2, \ldots, \mathbf{v}_n$ in $\mathcal{B}$ such that

$$\mathbf{v} = c_1\mathbf{v}_1 + c_2\mathbf{v}_2 + \ldots + c_n\mathbf{v}_n.$$

But this contradicts linear independence of $\mathcal{C}$ because $\mathcal{B} \subset \mathcal{C}$.

Choice (E) cannot possibly be true. It directly contradicts linear independence.

Thus, choice (D) must be correct. As we know from the remarks above $\mathbf{0}$ is not in $\mathcal{B}$. Hence, $\mathcal{D} := \{2v : v \in \mathcal{B}\}$ is disjoint from $\mathcal{B}$, and it is a basis as long as $\mathbb{F}$ doesn't have characteristic 2. $\quad\square$

Question 2.31. ────────────────────────

Recall the *Rational roots theorem* from Precalculus:

> Suppose $p(x) = a_n x^n + a_{n-1} x^{n-1} + \ldots + a_0$ is a polynomial such that $a_1, a_2, \ldots, a_n$ are integers. Then every rational root can be reduced to p/q, where p is an integer factor of a_0 and q is an integer factor of a_n.

Not much can be said about the numerator of a rational root of $9x^5 + ax^3 + b$ because we don't know the value of b, but the denominator must be a factor of 9. Four does not meet this criterion so $1/4$ cannot be a root. $\quad\square$

Question 2.32. ────────────────────────

The total number of ways 20 children can be lined up is 20!, half of which have Pat behind Lynn and half have Pat ahead of Lynn. Thus, exactly half of the total number of combinations have Pat ahead of Lynn. It follows that the total number of combinations with Pat ahead of Lynn is 20!/2. $\quad\square$

Question 2.33. ────────────────────────

There are a total of $\lfloor \frac{1,000}{30} \rfloor = \lfloor 33.\bar{3} \rfloor = 33$ integers between from 1 to 1,000 that are divisible by 30. A number is divisible by both 30 and 16 if and only if it is divisible by the least common multiple of 30 and 16, i.e. it is divisible by 240. There are a total of $\lfloor \frac{1,000}{240} \rfloor = \lfloor 4.1\bar{6} \rfloor = 4$ numbers from 1 to 1,000 divisible by 240. Thus, there are a total of $33 - 4 = 29$ integers from 1 to 1,000 that are divisible by 30 but not 16. $\quad\square$

Question 2.34. ————————————————————————

Choice (B) is not always true. The function f may not have a second derivative, and even if it does $\lim_{x \to \infty} f''(x)$ may not exist. Consider

$$f(x) := \int_1^{x^2} \frac{\sin t^2}{t^2} \, dt.$$

The second derivative of f is

$$f''(x) = 8 \cos x^4 - \frac{6 \sin x^4}{x^4},$$

which does not converge to a particular value as $x \to \infty$.

The necessity of choices (C), (D), and (E) is easily disproven by

$$f(x) := 1 - e^{-x}.$$

By the disjunctive syllogism, the correct answer must be (A). Let's prove it! We already know that $\lim_{x \to \infty} f'(x)$ exists or equivalently there is an L such that for every sequence $\{c_n\}_n$ where $\lim_{n \to \infty} c_n = \infty$ we have $\lim_{n \to \infty} f'(c_n) = L$. So we only need to find $\lim_{n \to \infty} f'(c_n)$ for one such sequence $\{c_n\}_n$. Let c_n be a number in $(n, n+1)$ such that

$$f'(c_n) = \frac{f(n+1) - f(n)}{n+1-n} = f(n+1) - f(n).$$

We are guarantied that c_n exists for all n because of the *mean value theorem*. Furthermore, it's clear $\lim_{n \to \infty} c_n = \infty$. Thus,

$$\begin{aligned} \lim_{x \to \infty} f'(x) &= \lim_{n \to \infty} f'(c_n) \\ &= \lim_{n \to \infty} f(n+1) - f(n) \\ &= 0. \end{aligned}$$

□

Question 2.35. ————————————————————————

To find the equation of a plane, we need a vector normal to the plane and a vector parallel to our plane that is constructed using an arbitrary point (x, y, z) on the plane.

We will find a normal vector first. If our plane is tangent to the surface $z = e^{-x} \sin y$ at $x = 0$ and $y = \pi/2$, then it has the same normal vector $\vec{n}$ at this point. From Calculus, we know a normal vector to the plane described by $z = f(x, y)$ is

$$n = (f_x(x, y), f_y(x, y), -1).$$

Let's compute the pieces:

$$\left.\frac{\partial z}{\partial x}\right|_{(0, \pi/2)} = -e^{-0} \sin \frac{\pi}{2} \quad \text{and} \quad \left.\frac{\partial z}{\partial y}\right|_{(0, \pi/2)} = e^{-0} \cos \frac{\pi}{2}$$

$$= -1 \qquad\qquad\qquad\qquad = 0.$$

Hence, $n := (-1, 0, -1)$ is normal to our plane.

The next piece of information we need is the vector parallel to our plane. When $x = 0$ and $y = \pi/2$,

$$z = e^{-0} \sin \frac{\pi}{2} = 1.$$

Therefore $(0, \pi/2, 1)$ is on our plane. It follows that $v := (x, y - \pi/2, z - 1)$ is parallel to our plane, whenever (x, y, z) is a point on our plane.

We know that the dot product of v and n is 0, because the vectors are orthogonal. That is,

$$v \cdot n = -x + 0 \left(y - \frac{\pi}{2} \right) - (z - 1)$$

$$= 0$$

Thus

$$x + z = 1.$$

$\square$

Question 2.36. ————————————————————————————
It's clear
$$\mu(x) = \frac{4+5+7+9+x}{5},$$
for all x. The median function is a little more tricky
$$\eta(x) = \begin{cases} 7 & \text{if } x \geq 7, \\ x & \text{if } 5 \leq x < 7, \\ 5 & \text{if } x < 5. \end{cases}$$

All that is left is to analyze what happens to η in each of its three cases:

Suppose $x \geq 7$ and $\mu(x) = \eta(x)$. Then
$$\frac{4+5+7+9+x}{5} = 7.$$

This implies $x = 10$.

Let $5 \leq x < 7$ and $\mu(x) = \eta(x)$. Then
$$\frac{4+5+7+9+x}{5} = x.$$

This implies $x = 25/4$.

Assume $x < 5$ and $\mu(x) = \eta(x)$. Then
$$\frac{4+5+7+9+x}{5} = 5.$$

This implies $x = 0$.

Thus, there are a total of three values of x that satisfy the criteria described in the question. $\qquad\square$

Question 2.37. ————————————————————————————
Recall
$$e := \sum_{k=0}^{\infty} \frac{1}{k!}.$$

Once the above is known, this problem becomes no more than a matter of rearranging, simplifying, and reindexing the given sum.

$$\sum_{k=1}^{\infty} \frac{k^2}{k!} = \sum_{k=1}^{\infty} \frac{k}{(k-1)!}$$

$$= \sum_{n=0}^{\infty} \frac{n+1}{n!}$$

$$= \sum_{n=0}^{\infty} \frac{n}{n!} + \sum_{n=0}^{\infty} \frac{1}{n!}$$

$$= 0 + \sum_{n=1}^{\infty} \frac{1}{(n-1)!} + \sum_{n=0}^{\infty} \frac{1}{n!}$$

$$= \sum_{m=0}^{\infty} \frac{1}{m!} + \sum_{n=0}^{\infty} \frac{1}{n!}$$

$$= 2 \sum_{n=0}^{\infty} \frac{1}{n!}$$

$$= 2e$$

□

Question 2.38.

One of the basic *integration properties* from Calculus is that if f and g are integrable and $f \le g$ on $[a, b]$ then

$$\int_a^b f(x) \, dx \le \int_a^b g(x) \, dx.$$

Also, note that $\sin t$ and $\cos t$ are non-negative when t is in $[0, \pi/2]$.

Let's examine our integrands. It's clear

$$\sin t \le \cos t$$

on $[0, \pi/4]$. It's also true that

$$\cos 2t \le \cos t$$

for t in $[0, \pi/4]$, because $\cos t$ is monotonically decreasing when t is in $[0, \pi/2]$ and the graph of $\cos 2t$ is the graph of $\cos t$ compressed horizontally to 1/2 its original length. Lastly, we have both

$$\cos^2 t \leq \cos t \quad \text{and} \quad \sin t \cos t \leq \cos t,$$

because $0 \leq \sin t \leq 1$ and $0 \leq \cos t \leq 1$ when t is in $[0, \pi/4]$. $\qquad \square$

Question 2.39. ────────────────────────────
Notice all these options, except (E), are in some sense describing the area between e^{-x} and x-axis when $0 \leq x \leq 10$. Let's call this region $\mathcal{R} := \{(x, y) : 0 \leq x \leq 10, 0 \leq y \leq e^{-x}\}$.

Choice (A) is an approximation of the area of $\mathcal{R}$ using n rectangles. The i-th rectangle has width $x_i - x_{i-1}$ and height $f(x_i)$, i.e. the height of the i-th rectangle is f evaluated at the right endpoint of the rectangle.

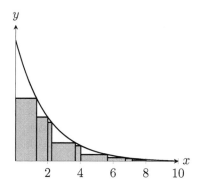

Choice (B) is an approximation of the area of $\mathcal{R}$ using n rectangles. The i-th rectangle has width $x_i - x_{i-1}$ and height $f(x_{i-1})$, i.e. the height of the i-th rectangle is f evaluated at the left endpoint of the rectangle.

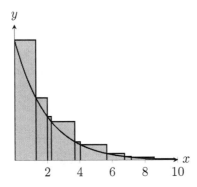

Choice (C) is an approximation of the area of $\mathcal{R}$ using n rectangles. The i-th rectangle has width $x_i - x_{i-1}$ and height $f\left(\frac{x_i + x_{i-1}}{2}\right)$, i.e. the height of the i-th rectangle is f evaluated at the midpoint of the rectangle.

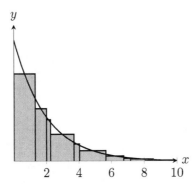

Choice (D) is the actual area of $\mathcal{R}$.

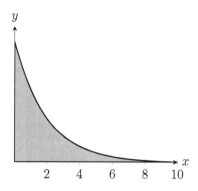

Choice (E) is clearly out because the area of $\mathcal{R}$ is greater than 0.

As the graphs above make clear, (B) is the correct answer. Generally, when f is monotonically decreasing, using the value of x at the left endpoint of each rectangle for the height $f(x)$ is an overestimate of the area under a curve. $\qquad$ $\square$

Question 2.40. ———————————————————————————
Coin tosses are an example of a *binomial distribution*. We need the following formula.

> Suppose we have a binomial distribution and the probability of one successful trial is p. Then the probability of exactly k successes in n independent trials is
> $$\binom{n}{k} p^k (1-p)^{n-k}.$$

Our task is to compute the probability that $k \geq 5$ trials end in the affirmative, when there are a total of $n = 8$ trials and the probability of each trial ending in the affirmative is $p = 1/2$. Thus, using the above formula and basic *probability properties* it follows that this event has probability

$$\binom{8}{5}\left(\frac{1}{2}\right)^8 + \binom{8}{6}\left(\frac{1}{2}\right)^8 + \binom{8}{7}\left(\frac{1}{2}\right)^8 + \binom{8}{8}\left(\frac{1}{2}\right)^8$$

$$= \frac{1}{256}\left(\binom{8}{5} + \binom{8}{6} + \binom{8}{7} + \binom{8}{8}\right)$$

$$= \frac{1}{256}\left(\frac{8!}{3!5!} + \frac{8!}{2!6!} + \frac{8!}{1!7!} + \frac{8!}{0!8!}\right)$$

$$= \frac{21}{16}\left(\frac{56}{336} + \frac{28}{336} + \frac{8}{336} + \frac{1}{336}\right)$$

$$= \frac{21}{16}\left(\frac{31}{112}\right)$$

$$= \frac{93}{256}.$$

□

Question 2.41.

We will use *second derivatives test* from Calculus.

Let $f : \mathbb{R}^2 \to \mathbb{R}$ have continuous second order partial derivatives in some $E \subseteq \mathbb{R}^2$. Suppose the point (a, b) in E is a critical point of f, i.e. $f_x(a, b) = 0$ and $f_y(a, b) = 0$. Define

$$H_f(x, y) := \det \begin{pmatrix} f_{xx}(x, y) & f_{xy}(x, y) \\ f_{yx}(x, y) & f_{yy}(x, y) \end{pmatrix}$$

$$= f_{xx}(x, y)f_{yy}(x, y) - [f_{xy}(x, y)]^2 .$$

- If $f_{xx}(a, b) > 0$ and $H_f(a, b) > 0$, then $f(a, b)$ is a relative minimum.

- If $f_{xx}(a, b) < 0$ and $H_f(a, b) > 0$, then $f(a, b)$ is a relative maximum.

- If $H_f(a, b) < 0$, then (a, b) is a saddle point.

- If $H_f(a, b) = 0$, then the test gives no information.

Let's compute our critical numbers. It's clear

$$f_x(x, y) = y - 3x^2 \quad \text{and} \quad f_y(x, y) = x - 3y^2.$$

Setting our partials equal to zero, and solving shows that our critical points are $(0,0)$ and $(1/3, 1/3)$.

Next, we compute our second order partial derivatives, which we will use to find our relative maximum.

$$f_{xx}(x,y) = -6x, \quad f_{xy}(x,y) = 1, \quad f_{yx}(x,y) = 1,$$
$$\text{and} \quad f_{yy}(x,y) = -6y,$$

which implies

$$H_f(x,y) = 36xy - 1.$$

It follows that

$$f_{xx}(1/3, 1/3) = -3 < 0 \quad \text{and} \quad H_f(1/3, 1/3) = 3 > 0.$$

Therefore, there is a relative maximum at $(1/3, 1/3)$. Note $H_f(0,0) = -1$, which means there is a saddle point when $x = y = 0$. $\quad\square$

Question 2.42.

This is tricky because C is so far from the origin in the southeast direction, that it makes D_3 far from the origin in the northeast direction. To alleviate this issue, let's scale our points by $1/2$ before we graph them, i.e. let's graph $A' = (-1/2, 1)$, $B' = (3, 2)$, and $C' = (1/2, -10)$. Since angles are preserved under contractions, this will not affect the result.

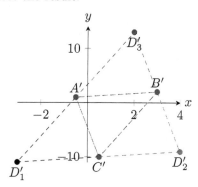

In case it's hard to see, our parallelograms are $\square A' D_1' C' B'$, $\square A' C' D_2' B'$, and $\square A' C' B' D_3'$. $\quad\square$

Question 2.43. ────────────────────────────────

After a quick glance, it's easy to that

$$\begin{pmatrix} 6 \\ 7 \\ 8 \end{pmatrix} = -\begin{pmatrix} 0 \\ 1 \\ 2 \end{pmatrix} + 2\begin{pmatrix} 3 \\ 4 \\ 5 \end{pmatrix}.$$

Since matrices are linear transformations, we have

$$A\begin{pmatrix} 6 \\ 7 \\ 8 \end{pmatrix} = A\left(-\begin{pmatrix} 0 \\ 1 \\ 2 \end{pmatrix} + 2\begin{pmatrix} 3 \\ 4 \\ 5 \end{pmatrix}\right)$$

$$= -A\begin{pmatrix} 0 \\ 1 \\ 2 \end{pmatrix} + 2A\begin{pmatrix} 3 \\ 4 \\ 5 \end{pmatrix}$$

$$= -\begin{pmatrix} 1 \\ 0 \\ 0 \end{pmatrix} + 2\begin{pmatrix} 0 \\ 1 \\ 0 \end{pmatrix}$$

$$= \begin{pmatrix} -1 \\ 2 \\ 0 \end{pmatrix}.$$

□

Question 2.44. ────────────────────────────────

Choice (A) is true.

$$\lim_{x \to 0^+} (\sqrt{x})^x = \lim_{x \to 0^+} e^{\frac{x \log x}{2}}$$

$$= e^{\lim_{x \to 0^+} \frac{\log x}{2/x}}$$

$$\overset{LH}{=} e^{\lim_{x \to 0^+} -x/2}$$

$$= 1,$$

where LH denotes the use of *L'Hôspital's rule*.

Choice (B) is clearly sound, because $(\sqrt{x})^x > \sqrt{x}$ when $x > 1$ and $\sqrt{x} \to \infty$ as $x \to \infty$.

Choice (C) is valid. It's a simple application of exponent rules; $(\sqrt{x})^x = \left(x^{1/2}\right)^x = x^{x/2}$. It's only over the complex domain that $x^{1/2}$ is a dubious statement.

Choice (D) is the lie. Let's compute the derivative.

$$\frac{d}{dx}x^{x/2} = \frac{d}{dx}e^{x\log(x)/2}$$

$$= e^{x\log(x)/2}\left(\frac{1}{2} + \frac{\log x}{2}\right)$$

$$= x^{x/2}\left(\frac{1}{2} + \frac{\log x}{2}\right).$$

Recall that $\lim_{x\to 0+}\log x = -\infty$. So it looks like $f'(x) < 0$ for x sufficiently small. Let's try $x = 1/e^2$:

$$\left(\frac{1}{e^2}\right)^{1/2e^2}\left(\frac{1}{2} + \frac{\log(1/e^2)}{2}\right) = \left(\frac{1}{e}\right)^{1/2e^2}\left(\frac{1}{2} - 1\right)$$

$$= -\frac{1}{2}\left(\frac{1}{e}\right)^{1/2e^2}$$

$$< 0$$

See the glossary if there are questions on any of the *logarithm properties* utilized above.

Choice (E) is true. We've already computed $f'(x)$, so $f''(x)$ is a simple application of the product rule.

$$\frac{d}{dx}\left(x^{x/2}\left(\frac{1}{2} + \frac{\log x}{2}\right)\right) = x^{x/2}\left(\frac{1}{2x}\right) + x^{x/2}\left(\frac{1}{2} + \frac{\log x}{2}\right)^2$$

The square in the second term guaranties the desired result. □

Question 2.45. ───────────────────────────────
The function $E(v(t))$ is miles traveled per gallon at velocity $v(t)$, so $1/E(v(t))$ must be gallons used per mile traveled at velocity $v(t)$. Hence,

$$dG = \frac{ds}{E(v(t))},$$

where dG is the infinitesimal number gallons of fuel used and ds is an infinitesimal distance traveled. Since

$$\frac{ds}{dt} = v(t),$$

it follows that
$$ds = v(t)\,dt.$$

Therefore
$$
\begin{aligned}
G &= \int_{t=0}^{4} dG \\
&= \int_{t=0}^{4} \frac{ds}{E(v(t))} \\
&= \int_{0}^{4} \frac{v(t)}{E(v(t))}\,dt.
\end{aligned}
$$

$\square$

Question 2.46. ———————————————————————————————

If α_1 and α_2 are the two zeros of a monic second degree polynomial $p(x)$, then
$$
\begin{aligned}
p(x) &= (x - \alpha_1)(x - \alpha_2) \\
&= x^2 - (\alpha_1 + \alpha_2)x + \alpha_1\alpha_2,
\end{aligned}
$$

so the coefficient of the term of degree 1 is the opposite of the sum of the two zeros. Note "monic" means the coefficient of the term of highest degree is 1.

With this in mind, let's compute the characteristic equation of our matrix
$$
\begin{aligned}
\det \begin{pmatrix} \lambda - \cos t & -\sin t \\ \sin t & \lambda - \cos t \end{pmatrix} &= (\lambda - \cos t)^2 + \sin t \\
&= \lambda - 2\lambda\cos t + \cos^2 t + \sin^2 t \\
&= \lambda - 2\lambda\cos t + 1.
\end{aligned}
$$

Thus, if $\lambda_1 + \lambda_2 = 1$, then $2\cos t = 1$. This implies $t = \pi/3$. See the glossary for a list of *sine and cosine values in quadrant I.* $\square$

Question 2.47. ────────────────────────────────

If the distance between x and y is less than $1/2$, then $|x - y| < 1/2$. Since x and y are uniformly distributed independent random variables the probability that $|x - y| < 1/2$ is simply the area of the region where this is true. Let's graph it! This breaks down into two cases.

Case I $x \geq y$: Then we graph $x - y < 1/2$ or the equivalent form $y > x - 1/2$. So we shade the the area between $y = x - 1/2$ and $y = x$ on the $[0, 1] \times [0, 1]$ box in the xy-plane, and we draw a dashed line where the former equation is and a solid line where the latter equation is.

Case II $y > x$: Then $y - x < 1/2$, which is equivalent to $y < x + 1/2$. So we shade the the the area between $y = x$ and $y = x + 1/2$ on the $[0, 1] \times [0, 1]$ box in the xy-plane, and we draw a dashed line where the latter equation is. The former equation has already been accounted for in case I.

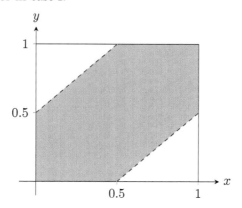

Hence, our area is $3/4$. □

Question 2.48. ────────────────────────────────

The boundary of $\{(x, y) : 0 \leq x \leq 1 \text{ and } 0 \leq y \leq 1\}$ will be sent to the boundary of our new region. So we break this problem up into four cases:

Case I $x = 0$: Then $u = y$, $v = 1 + y$, and $0 \leq y \leq 1$, which implies $v = 1 + u$, $0 \leq u \leq 1$, and $1 \leq v \leq 2$.

70

Case II $y = 0$: Then $u = x^{1/3}$, $v = 1$, and $0 \le x \le 1$, which implies $0 \le u \le 1$ when $v = 1$.

Case III $x = 1$: Then $u = 1 + y$, $v = 1 + y$, and $0 \le y \le 1$, which implies $u = v$, $1 \le u \le 2$, and $1 \le v \le 2$.

Case IV $y = 1$: Then $u = x^{1/3} + 1$, $v = 2$, and $0 \le x \le 1$, which implies $1 \le u \le 2$ when $v = 2$.

From here, the solution is clearly (A). $\qquad\square$

Question 2.49. ────────────────────────────
All of these are true. The first relationship follows easily after you recall that the graph of $f(x - 3)$ is the graph of $f(x)$ shifted right 3 places, so integrating over limits that are also shifted right 3 places doesn't affect the result. We could also let $u = x - 3$, which implies $du = dx$, and then substitute as needed on the right side of the equation. The second relationship follows from basic *integration properties* since

$$\int_a^3 f(x) \, dx - \int_b^3 f(x) \, dx = \int_a^3 f(x) \, dx + \int_3^b f(x) \, dx$$

$$= \int_a^b f(x) \, dx.$$

The third relationship follows from the fact that the graph of $f(3x)$ is the graph of $f(x)$ compressed horizontally by a third, so integrating over the interval scaled by $1/3$ will give a third the area (we get all the y-values, but in a third of the horizontal width). Alternatively, we could let $u = 3x$, which implies $du = 3 \, dx$, and substitute as needed on the right side of the equation. $\qquad\square$

Question 2.50. ────────────────────────────
If $(f(x))^2 = x^2$, then $|f(x)| = |x|$ or $f(x) = \pm x$. The arithmetic suggests the $\pm$ can change arbitrarily. However, f must be continuous, which means it's only possible for the sign to change at

$x = 0$. This is enough to conclude our four functions are:

$$f(x) = x, \quad f(x) = -x, \quad f(x) = \begin{cases} x & \text{if } x \in [0,1] \\ -x & \text{if } x \in [-1,0) \end{cases},$$

$$\text{and} \quad f(x) = \begin{cases} -x & \text{if } x \in [0,1] \\ x & \text{if } x \in [-1,0) \end{cases}.$$

□

Question 2.51. ───
From Calculus, we know

$$\sum_{k=1}^{\infty} \frac{(x+2y)^k}{k}$$

converges when $|x + 2y| < 1$ or $x + 2y = -1$. We can prove this using, for example, the *ratio test* and the *alternating series test*.

To graph D we break $|x + 2y| < 1$ up into two cases.

Case I $x + 2y \geq 0$: Then

$$-\frac{x}{2} \leq y \leq \frac{1-x}{2}.$$

Case II $x + 2y < 0$: Then

$$-\frac{x}{2} > y \leq -\frac{x+1}{2}.$$

Thus the interior of D is the open region between two parallel lines.

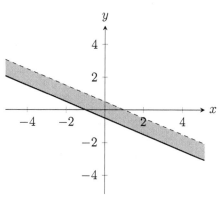

Question 2.52. ────────────────

First we convert our system into augmented matrix form, which yields

$$\left(\begin{array}{ccc|c} 1 & 1 & 1 & 0 \\ 1 & 2 & 3 & 0 \\ 1 & 3 & b & 0 \end{array} \right).$$

Using elementary row operations to change our matrix into row-echelon from gives us

$$\left(\begin{array}{ccc|c} 1 & 1 & 1 & 0 \\ 0 & 1 & 2 & 0 \\ 0 & 0 & b-5 & 0 \end{array} \right).$$

From here, it's clear that $b \neq 5$ permits only one solution, and $b = 5$ gives us infinitely many. ☐

Question 2.53. ────────────────

We need *Cauchy's residue theorem*.

> Suppose U is a simply connected open subset of and f a function holomorphic on $U \setminus \{a_1, a_2, \ldots, a_n\}$. Let C be a positively oriented simple closed curve whose image is contained in U such that $a_1, a_2, \ldots, a_n$ are inside of C. Then
>
> $$\int_C f(z)\, dz = 2\pi i \sum_{k=1}^{n} \text{Res}(f, a_k),$$
>
> where for a_k a pole of order m
>
> $$\text{Res}(f, a_k) = \frac{1}{(m-1)!} \lim_{z \to a_k} \frac{d^{m-1}}{dz^{m-1}} \left((z - a_k)^m f(z) \right).$$

The rest is an easy computation. The two poles of $\dfrac{1}{(z-1)(z+3)^2}$ are $z = 1$ and $z = -3$. However the latter pole is not contained

73

within C. Thus

$$\int_C \frac{dz}{(z-1)(z+3)^2} = 2\pi i \ \mathrm{Res}(f,1)$$

$$= 2\pi i \lim_{z \to 1} \frac{1}{(z+3)^2}$$

$$= \frac{\pi i}{8}.$$

$\square$

Question 2.54.
The first step is to set up the differential equation. Since the rate of change of water in the tank is the rate water enters minus the rate water leaves, it's clear

$$\frac{dV}{dt} = 1 - 0.25h.$$

Furthermore, $V(t) = 100h(t)$, so

$$\frac{dV}{dt} = 100\frac{dh}{dt}.$$

Hence,

$$100\frac{dh}{dt} = 1 - 0.25h.$$

Separating variables gives us

$$\frac{dh}{h-4} = -0.0025 \ dt.$$

Integrating both sides and solving for h yields

$$h(t) = Ce^{-0.0025t} + 4.$$

Thus,

$$\lim_{t \to \infty} V(t) = \lim_{t \to \infty} 100h(t)$$

$$= \lim_{t \to \infty} 100\left(Ce^{-0.0025t} + 4\right)$$

$$= 400.$$

$\square$

Question 2.55. ———————————————————————

Property I is always false. Because $f'(0)$ is negative and f' is continuous, f is decreasing on some interval starting at $x = 0$.

Property II is true. Suppose for the sake of contradiction that f has zeros z_1 and z_2 and $z_1 < z_2$. We will prove that f' also has two zeros.

Let's find the zeros of f'. From Calculus, we know f' is 0 when relative extrema occur, assuming f' is defined. Furthermore, the *first derivative test* tells us a local minimum occurs when f goes from decreasing to increasing. Since $f(0)$ and $f'(0)$ are negative, f is decreasing and negative on some interval. However, f begins to increase at some point, because the graph of f hits the x-axis when $x = z_1$. Thus there is some value $a_1 < z_1$ such that $f'(a_1) = 0$. We are guaranteed an a_2 between z_1 and z_2 such that $f'(a_2) = 0$, because of the *mean value theorem* applied to the closed interval $[z_1, z_2]$.

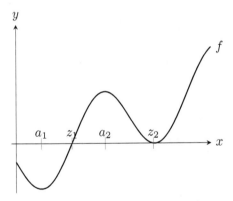

Via an identical argument, f' having two zeros implies that f'' has two zeros, which is a contradiction. Therefore f only has one zero.

Property III is true. Suppose for the sake of contradiction that f is bounded. Since f' has only one zero, f is monotonically increasing for large values of x. Then there is an N such that

$$\lim_{x \to \infty} f(x) = N.$$

By the *mean value theorem* there exists some b_n in $(n, n+1)$ such

75

that
$$f'(b_n) = \frac{f(n+1) - f(n)}{n-1-n} = f(n+1) - f(n).$$

This implies

$$\lim_{n\to\infty} f'(b_n) = \lim_{n\to\infty} f(n+1) - f(n)$$
$$= N - N$$
$$= 0.$$

Thus,
$$\lim_{x\to\infty} f'(x) = 0,$$

since f' is monotonically increasing for large values and $b_n \to \infty$ as $n \to \infty$. But applying an identical argument as above to f' instead of f implies f'' is bounded which is a contradiction of a stated hypothesis. $\square$

Question 2.56.

For all of the counter examples, assume $d : \mathbb{R}^2 \to \mathbb{R}$ is the Euclidian metric on $\mathbb{R}$, i.e. $d(x,y) := |x - y|$. A definition of a *metric* is located in the glossary.

The function $4 + d$ is not a metric, because the distance between a point and itself is not 0. Consider $(4+d)(1,1) = 4 + d(1,1) = 4 \neq 0$.

The function $e^d - 1$ is not a metric, because the triangle inequality fails to hold. Consider $e^{d(\log 3, 0)} - 1 = 2$ and $e^{d(\log 3, \log 2)} - 1 + e^{d(\log 2, 0)} - 1 = 3/2 - 1 + 2 - 1 = 3/2$. See the glossary if you have questions about the *logarithm properties* used.

The function $d - |d|$ is not a metric, because the distance between non-equal points is 0. Consider $(d - |d|)(1,0) = d(1,0) - |d(1,0)| = 1 - 1 = 0$.

The function d^2 is not a metric, because it doesn't satisfy the tri-angle inequality criterion. Consider $(d^2)(1,0) = (d(1,0))^2 = 1$ and $d^2(1,1/2) + d^2(1/2,0) = (1/2)^2 + (1/2)^2 = 1/2$.

By the processes of elimination $\sqrt{d}$ must be a metric, but let's prove it! Non-negativity and symmetry follow directly from d being a metric, which means all we need to prove is the triangle inequality. It's true that

$$\sqrt{x+y} \le \sqrt{x} + \sqrt{y}$$

for x and y non-negative; to prove this, simply square both sides and cancel as needed. With this in mind, it follows that

$$\sqrt{d(x,y)} \le \sqrt{d(x,z) + d(z,y)}$$
$$\le \sqrt{d(x,z)} + \sqrt{d(z,y)}.$$

$\square$

Question 2.57.

See the glossary for a definition of a *ring*. Note that a subring U for a ring R is simply a ring such that $U \subseteq R$.

Set I is a subring, since the sum, difference, and product of polynomials with no linear term have no linear term. It's clear that both the additive identity of 0 and multiplicative identity 1 are still in our ring. The other criteria necessary for a ring clearly hold.

The set described by II is not a subring, because it is not closed under addition. Both $x^2 + x$ and $-x^2$ have even degree, but $(x^2 + x) + (-x^2) = x$ has odd degree.

Set III must be a subring. Since $\mathbb{Q}$ is a subfield of $\mathbb{R}$, there is no way for our third set to fail the axioms. $\square$

Question 2.58.

Property I is true. The set S is connected, since the image of a connected set under a continuous map is connected.

The necessity of property II is debunked by $f(x) := 1$, because $S = \{f(c) : 0 < c < 1\} = \{1\}$ is closed.

Property III is false. The function f is continuous on all of $\mathbb{R}$. So $S \subseteq f[0,1]$, because $(0,1) \subset [0,1]$ and f is defined at 0 and 1. The set $f[0,1]$ is *compact* because the image of a compact set under a continuous function is compact. Therefore $f[0,1]$ is bounded via an application of the *Heine-Borel theorem*. It follows that S is also bounded. $\square$

Question 2.59. ─────────────────────────────────────
The set $\{x^3, x^5, x^9\}$ has two distinct elements. That means
$$x^9 = x^3, \ x^9 = x^5, \ \text{or } x^5 = x^3.$$
This implies
$$x^6 = 1, \ x^4 = 1, \ \text{or } x^2 = 1,$$
where 1 is the identity element in our *group*.

By *Lagrange's theorem* the order of a subgroup must divide the order of the group. However, 2 and 4 do not divide 15, which means if $x^4 = 1$ or $x^2 = 1$ were true $x = 1$ otherwise $\langle x \rangle$ would have order 2 or 4, an impossibility. But $x = 1$ cannot be either because it contradicts the fact that $\{x^3, x^5, x^9\}$ has two distinct elements. Thus,
$$x^6 = 1.$$
It follows that $\langle x \rangle$ has order 3, since 3 is the only common factor of 6 and 15 other than 1. Furthermore,
$$\langle x^{13} \rangle = \{x^{13n} : n \text{ is a positive integer}\}$$
also has order 3, because 13 does not divide 15. $\qquad\qquad\square$

Question 2.60. ─────────────────────────────────────
Property I is legit. Consider the following argument:
$$s + s = (s + s)^2$$
$$= s^2 + s^2 + s^2 + s^2$$
$$= s + s + s + s.$$
Adding $-s + -s$ to both sides yields the desired result.

Property II is valid; $(s + t)^2 = s + t = s^2 + t^2$.

Property III is also true. From property I, we know $s + s = 0$, which implies $s = -s$. Furthermore,
$$s + t = (s + t)^2$$
$$= s^2 + ts + st + t^2$$
$$= s + st + ts + st + t.$$

Adding $s+t$ to both sides gives us $st + ts = 0$. Hence, $st = -ts = ts$.

$\square$

Question 2.61.

The first step is to factor. It's clear

$$p^4 - 1 = (p-1)(p+1)(p^2+1).$$

Since p is a prime greater than 5, we can be confident that it is odd. Hence, both $p-1$, $p+1$, and p^2+1 are even. Furthermore, either $p-1$ or $p+1$ is divisible by 4, because every other even number is divisible by 4. It follows that $4 \cdot 2 \cdot 2 = 16$ divides $p^4 - 1$.

The numbers $p-1$, p, and $p+1$ are consecutive and in a list of three consecutive numbers one is always divisible by 3. Since p is a prime greater than 5, we can conclude either $p-1$ or $p+1$ is divisible by 3. So far we have $16 \cdot 3 = 48$ divides $p^4 - 1$.

Furthermore, *Fermat's little theorem* says

$$a^{q-1} \equiv 1 \pmod{q},$$

when q is a prime that does not divide a. It follows that $p^4 \equiv 1 \pmod 5$, or equivalently 5 divides $p^4 - 1$. Thus, $48 \cdot 5 = 240$ divides $p^4 - 1$.

We have not concluded that this is the largest number that divides $p^4 - 1$. However, 250 is our largest choice, which is sufficient for the GRE.

$\square$

Question 2.62.

We could compute the third derivative and use *Taylor's theorem* to obtain the result, but finding the third derivative of $(1+x)^3(2+x^2)^{10}$ is computationally intensive. Instead, recall :

$$(x+y)^n = \sum_{k=0}^{n} \binom{n}{k} x^{n-k} y^k.$$

Thus,

$$(1+x)^3(2+x^2)^{10} = \left(\binom{3}{0} + \binom{3}{1}x + \binom{3}{2}x^2\right.$$

$$+ \binom{3}{3}x^3\right)\left(\binom{10}{0}2^{10} + \binom{10}{1}2^9x^2\right.$$

$$\left. + \ldots + \binom{10}{10}x^{20}\right)$$

$$= (1 + 3x + 3x^2 + x^3)(2^{10} + 10 \cdot 2^9 x^2$$

$$+ 55 \cdot 2^8 x^4 + \ldots + x^{20})$$

For polynomials $a_0 + a_1 x + \ldots + a_n x^n$ and $b_0 + b_1 x + \cdots + b_m x^m$, the product is

$$(a_0 + a_1 x + \ldots + a_n x^n)(b_0 + b_1 x + \cdots + b_m x^m)$$

$$= \sum_{k=0}^{m+n} \left(\sum_{i+j=k} a_i b_j\right) x^k,$$

where $i = 0, 1, \ldots, n$ and $j = 0, 1, \ldots, m$. In particular, the coefficient in front of x^k is

$$\sum_{i+j=k} a_i b_j,$$

where $i = 0, 1, \ldots, n$ and $j = 0, 1, \ldots, m$.

Hence, the coefficient in front of x^3 will be

$$3 \cdot 10 \cdot 2^9 + 2^{10} = (30 + 2) \, 2^9$$

$$= 2^5 \cdot 2^9$$

$$= 2^{14}.$$

$\square$

Question 2.63. ─────────────────────────

Let's list the obvious first:

$$\lim_{x \to -\infty} x^{12} = \infty, \qquad 0^{12} = 0, \qquad \lim_{x \to \infty} x^{12} = \infty,$$

$$\lim_{x \to -\infty} 2^x = 0, \qquad 2^0 = 1, \qquad \lim_{x \to \infty} 2^x = \infty,$$

and

$$\lim_{x \to -\infty} 2^x - x^{12} = \infty.$$

Furthermore, we know 2^x increases monotonically for all x in $\mathbb{R}$, and x^{12} decreases monotonically when $x \leq 0$ and increases monotonically when $x \geq 0$. So we can be confident that both graphs behave relatively well.

We're ready to make our conclusions:

It's clear the graph of x^{12} starts above the graph of 2^x because $x^{12} \to \infty$ as $x \to -\infty$ and $2^x \to 0$ as $x \to -\infty$. However, the graphs intersect for one value of x in $(-\infty, 0)$ because $2^0 = 1 > 0^{12} = 0$. There is only one such x in $(-\infty, 0)$ due to the monotonicity of both graphs.

There is another intersection on the interval $(0, 2)$, because 2^{12} is greater than 2^2. This is the only intersection because we know how both graphs more-or-less look on the interval $(0, 2)$.

Lastly, 2^x eventually gets bigger that x^{12}, so there must be one more intersection. This is the last intersection because 2^x grows faster than x^{12} when $2^x > x^{12}$ and x is positive.

It follows that there are a total of three points where the graphs intersection. To appeal a bit to intuition, consider the graphs $y = 2^x$ and $y = x^2$ which are shown on the next page. The behaviors of these two graphs are very similar to that of 2^x and x^{12}.

□

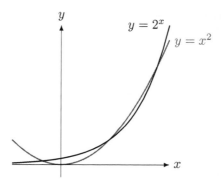

$y = 2^x$

$y = x^2$

Question 2.64.

Property I is true. Since f is continuous, $f[0,1]$ is *compact*, and by the *Heine-Borel theorem* also closed and bounded. Hence,

$$M = \sup_{x \in [0,1]} \{f(x)\} \qquad \text{and} \qquad m = \inf_{x \in [0,1]} \{f(x)\},$$

for some m and M in $\mathbb{R}$. Let $C := M - m$, and the result follows.

Property II is also legitimate. Recall that if f has a compact domain, then its continuity implies it has *uniform continuity*. Thus for all $\varepsilon > 0$, there exists a $\delta > 0$ such that $|x - y| < \delta$ implies $|f(x) - f(y)| < \varepsilon$. Pick $\varepsilon = 1$ and the conclusion follows.

Property III is false. It's called *"Lipschitz continuity"*, and claiming a function is Lipschitz continuous is a stronger statement about the function than continuity is. Let's find a function that is continuous on $[0,1]$ but not Lipschitz continuous. To make our task a bit easier, notice that, by dividing both sides by $|x - y|$, Lipschitz continuity is equivalent to saying there is a constant E such that

$$\left| \frac{f(x) - f(y)}{x - y} \right| \leq E$$

for all x and y in $[0,1]$ and $x \neq y$. Now consider $f(x) := \sqrt{x}$, which is continuous on $[0,1]$;

$$\left| \frac{f(x) - f(y)}{x - y} \right| = \left| \frac{\sqrt{x} - \sqrt{y}}{x - y} \right|$$

$$= \left| \frac{1}{\sqrt{x} + \sqrt{y}} \right|$$

82

goes to infinity as x and y independently go to zero, so the ratio cannot be bounded. $\square$

Question 2.65. ──────────────────
Suppose α_1, α_2, and α_3 are zeros of a third degree monic (i.e. the coefficient in front of x^3 is 1) polynomial q. Then

$$q(x) = (x - \alpha_1)(x - \alpha_2)(x - \alpha_3)$$
$$= x^3 - (\alpha_1 + \alpha_2 + \alpha_3)x^2 + (\alpha_1\alpha_2 + \alpha_1\alpha_3 + \alpha_2\alpha_3)x$$
$$- \alpha_1\alpha_2\alpha_3.$$

Since $p(-3) = p(2) = 0$,

$$p(x) = (x + 3)(x - 2)\left(x - \frac{c}{6}\right).$$

This implies

$$p'(x) = (x - 2)\left(x - \frac{c}{6}\right) + (x + 3)\left(x - \frac{c}{6}\right) + (x + 3)(x - 2).$$

So

$$p'(-3) = 15 + \frac{5c}{6} < 0.$$

Hence,

$$c < -24.$$

$\square$

Question 2.66. ──────────────────
Using *Green's theorem*, it follows that

$$\oint_C -2y\, dx + x^2\, dy = \iint\limits_{\{(x,y):\ x^2+y^2\leq 9\}} \frac{\partial}{\partial x}(x^2) - \frac{\partial}{\partial x}(-2y)\ dA$$

$$= \iint\limits_{\{(x,y):\ x^2+y^2\leq 9\}} 2x + 2\ dA$$

$$= \iint\limits_{\{(r,\theta):\ 0\leq r\leq 3,\ 0\leq\theta\leq 2\pi\}} (2r\cos\theta + 2)\ r\,dr\,d\theta$$

$$= 18\pi.$$

83

Note we switched to *polar coordinates* above, which required the following two formulae

$$x = r\cos\theta \quad \text{and} \quad dA = rdrd\theta.$$

$\square$

Glossary

Alternating series test Consider the infinite series $\sum a_n$ and suppose
$$a_n = (-1)^n b_n,$$
where b_n is positive and decreases monotonically. Then $\sum a_n$ converges if and only if
$$\lim_{n \to \infty} b_n = 0.$$

Antiderivatives Useful antiderivatives.

- $\displaystyle\int u^n \, du = \frac{u^{n+1}}{n+1} + C, \quad n \neq -1$

- $\displaystyle\int e^u \, du = e^u + C$

- $\displaystyle\int \frac{du}{u} = \log |u| + C$

- $\displaystyle\int \sin u \, du = -\cos u + C$

- $\displaystyle\int \cos u \, du = \sin u + C$

- $\displaystyle\int \tan u \, du = -\log |\cos u| + C$

- $\displaystyle\int \frac{du}{1 + u^2} = \text{Arctan } u + C$

Arc length

- Curve described in terms of a function: Suppose $y = f(x)$. Then the arc length from $x = a$ to $x = b$ is

$$\int_a^b \sqrt{1 + \left(\frac{dx}{dt}\right)^2}\, dx.$$

- Curve described in terms of a third parameter: Suppose $x = f(t)$ and $y = g(t)$ describe a curve. Then the arc length from $t = a$ to $t = b$ is

$$\int_a^b \sqrt{\left(\frac{dx}{dt}\right)^2 + \left(\frac{dy}{dt}\right)^2}\, dt.$$

- Curve described in polar coordinates: Suppose $r = f(\theta)$. Then the arc length from $\theta = \alpha$ to $\theta = \beta$ is

$$\int_\alpha^\beta \sqrt{r^2 + \left(\frac{dr}{d\theta}\right)^2}\, d\theta.$$

Basis The set $\mathcal{B}$ is a basis of a vector space V over a field $\mathbb{F}$ if and only if

- The set $\mathcal{B}$ is nonempty,

- Every element in V can be written as a linear combination of elements in $\mathcal{B}$,

- The elements of $\mathcal{B}$ are linearly independent.

Binomial distribution Suppose n independent trials are conducted, each of which can either end in success or failure. Let p be the probability success. Then the probability of exactly k trials ending in success is

$$\binom{n}{k} p^k (1 - p)^{n-k}.$$

Furthermore, in a binomial distribution

- The mean is $\mu = np$

- The variance is $\sigma^2 = np(1-p)$

- The standard deviation is $\sigma = \sqrt{np(1-p)}$

Cardinal arithmetic Let A and B be sets.

- $|A| + |B| = |A \coprod B|$ where $A \coprod B$ denotes the disjoint union of A and B.

- $|A||B| = |A \times B|$.

- $\left|\{f \mid f : A \to B\}\right| = |B|^{|A|}$.

- $|A| \cdot |B| = \sup\{|A|, |B|\}$ if $|A|$ or $|B|$ is an infinite cardinal.

Cauchy's residue theorem Suppose U is a simply connected open subset of $\mathbb{C}$ and f is a function holomorphic on $U \setminus \{a_1, a_2, \ldots, a_n\}$. Let C is a positively oriented simple closed curve whose image is contained in U, and suppose $a_1, a_2, \ldots, a_n$ are inside of C. Then

$$\int_C f(z)\, dz = 2\pi i \sum_{k=1}^{n} \operatorname{Res}(f, a_k),$$

where for a_k a pole of order m

$$\operatorname{Res}(f, a_k) = \frac{1}{(m-1)!} \lim_{z \to c} \frac{d^{m-1}}{dz^{m-1}} \left((z - a_k)^m f(z)\right).$$

http://en.wikipedia.org/wiki/Residue_Theorem

Compact Consider the set X under some topology. A collection $\mathcal{U}$ of open sets is said to be an "open cover" if and only if

$$X \subseteq \bigcup_{U \in \mathcal{U}} U.$$

The set X is compact if and only if every open cover $\mathcal{U}$ has a finite subcover $\{U_1, U_2, \ldots, U_n\} \subseteq \mathcal{U}$ such that

$$X \subseteq U_1 \cup U_2 \cup \ldots \cup U_n.$$

Dense Suppose A and B are subsets of a topological space X. We say A is dense in B if and only if $\mathrm{cl}(A) = B$. In other words, every point of B is a limit point of A or an element of A.

Derivatives have no "simple discontinuities" Suppose f is differentiable on the open interval (a, b) and c is in (a, b). Then

$$\lim_{x \to c^-} f'(x) = \lim_{x \to c^+} f'(x),$$

if both limits exist. See *Principles of Mathematical Analysis* by Rudin 3rd edition page 109.

Descartes's rule of signs Suppose $f(x) = a_n x^n + a_{n-1} x^{n-1} + \ldots + a_1 x + a_0$. Then the number of positive zeros of f is equal to the number of sign changes of $f(x)$ or is an even number less. Furthermore, the number of negative zeros of f is equal to the number of sign changes of $f(-x)$ or is an even number less.

e

$$e := \sum_{k=0}^{\infty} \frac{1}{k!} = \lim_{n \to \infty} \left(\frac{n+1}{n} \right)^n.$$

Euler's formula $e^{i\theta} = \cos\theta + i\sin\theta$ for all θ in $\mathbb{C}$.

Extreme value theorem Let f be a continuous function from a compact set X to $\mathbb{R}$. Then there exist x_1 and x_2 in X such that

$$f(x_1) = \sup_{x \in X} \{f(x)\} \quad \text{and} \quad f(x_2) = \inf_{x \in X} \{f(x)\}.$$

Fermat's little theorem Suppose p is a prime number and a is an integer. Then
$$a^p \equiv a \pmod{p}.$$

Furthermore, if p does not divide a, then

$$a^{p-1} \equiv 1 \pmod{p}.$$

http://en.wikipedia.org/wiki/Fermat's_little_theorem

First derivative test Suppose $f : \mathbb{R} \to \mathbb{R}$ is continuous on the open interval (a, b) and differentiable on $(a, b) \setminus \{c\}$.

- If $f'(x) > 0$ for x in (a, c) and $f'(x) < 0$ for x in (c, b), then $f(c)$ is a relative maximum.

- If $f'(x) < 0$ for x in (a, c) and $f'(x) > 0$ for x in (c, b), then $f(c)$ is a relative minimum.

Fundamental counting principle Suppose there are n_1 ways to complete one activity, and n_2 ways of completing another independent activity. Then there are

$$n_1 \cdot n_2$$

ways to complete both. More generally, if there are n_i ways to complete the i-th independent activity, where $i = 1, 2, \ldots, m$ then there are

$$\prod_{i=1}^{m} n_i$$

ways to complete all m activities.

Fundamental theorem of Calculus Suppose f is continuous on $[a, b]$. Then

$$\int_a^b f(x) \, dx = F(b) - F(a),$$

where $F'(x) = f(x)$.

Fundamental theorem of finitely generated abelian groups Let G be a finitely generated abelian group. Then it is isomorphic to an expression of the form

$$\mathbb{Z}^k \times \mathbb{Z}_{p_1^{\alpha_1}} \times \mathbb{Z}_{p_2^{\alpha_2}} \times \ldots \mathbb{Z}_{p_n^{\alpha_m}},$$

where $k, \alpha_1, \alpha_2, \ldots, \alpha_m$ are whole number and $p_1, p_2, \ldots, p_m$ are primes which are not necessarily distinct. Alternatively, G is isomorphic to an expression of the form

$$\mathbb{Z}^k \times \mathbb{Z}_{r_1} \times \mathbb{Z}_{r_2} \times \ldots \times \mathbb{Z}_{r_n},$$

where $k, r_1, r_2, \ldots, r_n$ are whole numbers and r_i divides r_{i+1} for all $i = 1, 2, \ldots, n-1$. Note that k and each r_i are uniquely determined by G.

Green's theorem Let C be a positively oriented, piecewise smooth, simple closed curve in the xy-plane, and let D be the region bounded by C. Suppose L and M are functions of x and y and have continuous partial derivatives on an open region containing D, then

$$\oint_C L\ dx + M\ dy = \iint_D \frac{\partial M}{\partial x} - \frac{\partial L}{\partial y}\ dA,$$

where the path of integration along C is counterclockwise. http://en.wikipedia.org/wiki/Green_theorem

Group The set G together with a binary operation $\cdot$ is a group if and only if the following properties of G and $\cdot$ hold:

- Closed: a and b in G implies $a \cdot b$ in G.

- Associative: for all a, b, and c in G, we have $(a \cdot b) \cdot c = a \cdot (b \cdot c)$.

- Contains the identity element: there is an element e such that $e \cdot a = a \cdot e = a$ for all a in G.

- Contains inverse elements: for all a in G there is a^{-1} such that $a \cdot a^{-1} = a^{-1} \cdot a = e$.

http://en.wikipedia.org/wiki/Group_(mathematics)

Heine-Borel theorem A set in $\mathbb{R}^n$ is closed and bounded if and only if it is compact.

Inclusion-exclusion principle For finite sets $A_1, A_2, \ldots, A_n$, the following holds

$$\left| \bigcup_{i=1}^n A_i \right| = \sum_{i=1}^n |A_i| - \sum_{1 \le i < j \le n} |A_i \cap A_j|$$
$$+ \sum_{1 \le i < j < k \le n} |A_i \cap A_j \cap A_k| - \cdots$$
$$+ (-1)^{n-1} |A_1 \cap \cdots \cap A_n|.$$

http://en.wikipedia.org/wiki/Inclusionexclusion_principle

Integration by parts Suppose u and v are differentiable functions of x. Then

$$\int u \; dv = uv - \int v \; du.$$

Integration properties Suppose f and g are integrable real valued functions over $[a, b]$. Let α and β be in $\mathbb{R}$. Then

- $\int_a^b \alpha f(x) + \beta g(x) \; dx = \alpha \int_a^b f(x) \; dx + \beta \int_a^b g(x) \; dx$

- $\int_a^b f(x) \; dx = - \int_b^a f(x) \; dx$

- $\int_a^b f(x) \; dx = \int_a^c f(x) \; dx + \int_c^b f(x) \; dx$

- $\int_a^b f(x) \; dx \leq \int_a^b g(x) \; dx$ if $f(x) \leq g(x)$ for x in $[a, b]$

Intermediate value theorem Let f be a real-valued continuous function on the closed interval $[a, b]$. For each y between $f(a)$ and $f(b)$, there is a c in $[a, b]$ such that $f(c) = y$.

Inverse of a 2×2 invertible matrix Suppose $A := \begin{pmatrix} a & b \\ c & d \end{pmatrix}$ is invertible. Then

$$A^{-1} = \frac{1}{ad - bc} \begin{pmatrix} d & -b \\ -c & a \end{pmatrix}.$$

L'Hôspital's rule Let f and g be functions differentiable on $(a, b) \setminus \{c\}$, and $g(x) \neq 0$ for all x in $(a, b) \setminus \{c\}$, where c is in (a, b). Assume $\lim_{x \to c} f(x) = \lim_{x \to c} g(x) = 0$ or $\lim_{x \to c} f(x) = \lim_{x \to c} g(x) = \pm\infty$. Then

$$\lim_{x \to c} \frac{f(x)}{g(x)} = \lim_{x \to c} \frac{f'(x)}{g'(x)}.$$

Lagrange's theorem For any finite group G, the order of every subgroup H of G divides the order of G. http://en. wikipedia.org/wiki/Lagrange's_theorem_(group_theory)

Law of cosines Consider $\triangle ABC$ shown below.

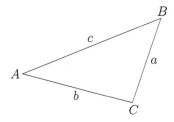

Then

- $a^2 = b^2 + c^2 - 2bc \cos A$
- $b^2 = a^2 + c^2 - 2ac \cos B$
- $c^2 = a^2 + b^2 - 2ab \cos C$

Least upper bound The value x is the least upper bound of a set A if and only if the following criteria are satisfied:

- $x \geq a$ for all a in A,
- $y \geq a$ for all a in A implies $y \geq x$.

Lipschitz continuity Let (X, ρ) and (Y, σ) be metric spaces. A function $f : X \to Y$ is Lipschitz continuous if and only if there exists a real constant $C \geq 0$ such that for x_1 and x_2 in X

$$\sigma(f(x_1), f(x_2)) \leq C\rho(x_1, x_2).$$

http://en.wikipedia.org/wiki/Lipschitz_continuity

Logarithm properties The GRE assumes log is base e <u>not</u> base 10.

- $\int \dfrac{du}{u} = \log |u| + C$
- $\log x = y \iff e^y = x$
- $\log 1 = 0$
- $\log e = 1$
- $\log(xy) = \log x + \log y$
- $\log(x/y) = \log x - \log y$

- $\log x^y = y \log x$

Mean value theorem Let f be continuous on the closed interval $[a, b]$ and differentiable on the open interval (a, b). Then there is some c in (a, b) such that

$$f'(c) = \frac{f(b) - f(a)}{b - a}.$$

`http://en.wikipedia.org/wiki/Mean_value_theorem`

Method of Lagrange multipliers Suppose $f(x, y, z)$ and $g(x, y, z)$ have continuous first order partial derivatives, and there is a constant k such that $g(x, y, z) = k$. Then relative extrema of f occur at the points (x, y, z) that satisfy

$$f_x(x, y, x) = \lambda g_x(x, y, z), \qquad f_y(x, y, z) = \lambda g_y(x, y, z),$$
$$\text{and} \quad f_z(x, y, z) = \lambda g_z(x, y, z)$$

for some λ in $\mathbb{R}$.

Metric A metric on a set X is a function $d : X \times X \to \mathbb{R}$ such that for all x, y, and z in X the following hold:

- Non-negativity: $d(x, y) \geq 0$ and $d(x, y) = 0$ if and only if $x = y$

- Symmetry: $d(x, y) = d(y, x)$

- Triangle inequality: $d(x, z) \leq d(x, y) + d(y, z)$

Necessary and sufficient condition for a function to be analytic The function $f(z) = u(x, y) + iv(x, y)$ is analytic if and only if

$$\frac{\partial u}{\partial x} = \frac{\partial v}{\partial y} \quad \text{and} \quad \frac{\partial u}{\partial y} = -\frac{\partial v}{\partial x}.$$

Newton's binomial theorem

$$(x + y)^n = \sum_{k=0}^{n} \binom{n}{k} x^{n-k} y^k.$$

Pigeonhole principle Suppose we want to put n items into m slots. Then there must be at least one slot that contains at least $\lceil n/m \rceil$ items and there must be a slot that holds no more than $\lfloor n/m \rfloor$.

Polar coordinates Conversions between polar and rectangular coordinates.

$$x = r\cos\theta, \quad y = r\sin\theta, \quad r^2 = x^2 + y^2, \quad \text{and} \quad dA = rdrd\theta.$$

Probability properties Let X be the sample space, and A and B be events in X.

- $P(X) = 1$
- $P(\varnothing) = 0$
- $0 \le P(A) \le 1$
- $P(X \setminus A) = 1 - P(A)$
- $P(B) \le P(A)$ if $B \subseteq A$
- $P(A \setminus B) = P(A) - P(A \cap B)$
- $P(A \cup B) = P(A) + P(B) - P(A \cap B)$
- $P(A \cap B) = P(A) \cdot P(B)$ if A and B are independent events

Pythagorean identities Suppose θ is in $\mathbb{R}$. Then

$$\cos^2\theta + \sin^2\theta = 1, \quad 1 + \tan^2\theta = \sec^2\theta, \quad \text{and} \quad 1 + \cot^2\theta = \csc^2\theta.$$

Rank nullity theorem Suppose V is a finite dimensional vector space and let $T : V \to W$ be a linear map. Then

$$\text{nullity}(T) + \text{rank}(T) = \dim(V)$$

Ratio test Consider the series $S := \sum_{n=1}^{\infty} a_n$ and the limit $L := \lim_{n \to \infty} \left| \frac{a_{n+1}}{a_n} \right|$.

- If $L < 1$ then the S converges absolutely.
- If $L > 1$ then S does not converge.

94

- If $L = 1$ or L doesn't exist, then the test is inconclusive.

Rational roots theorem Suppose $p(x) = a_n x^n + a_{n-1} x^{n-1} + \ldots + a_0$ is a polynomial such that $a_1, a_2, \ldots, a_n$ are integers. Then every rational root can be reduced to p/q, where p is an integer factor of a_0 and q is an integer factor of a_n.

Ring A set R is a ring if and only if it is an abelian group under $+$ and the following properties of R and $\cdot$ hold

- Associativity: $(a \cdot b) \cdot c = a \cdot (b \cdot c)$ for all a, b, and c in R.

- Contains a multiplicative identity: There is an element 1 in R such that $a \cdot 1 = a$ and $1 \cdot a = a$.

- Distributive on the right: $a \cdot (b + c) = a \cdot b + a \cdot c$ for all a, b, and c in R.

- Distributive on the left: $(b + c) \cdot a = b \cdot a + c \cdot a$ for all a, b, and c in R.

http://en.wikipedia.org/wiki/Ring_(mathematics)

Schröder-Berstein theorem If $|A| \leq |B|$ and $|B| \leq |A|$, then $|A| = |B|$.

Second derivatives test Suppose that the function $f : \mathbb{R}^2 \to \mathbb{R}$ has continuous second order partial derivatives in some $E \subseteq \mathbb{R}^2$. Suppose the point (a, b) in E is a critical point, i.e. $f_x(a, b) = 0$ and $f_y(a, b) = 0$. Define

$$H_f(x, y) := \det \begin{pmatrix} f_{xx}(x, y) & f_{xy}(x, y) \\ f_{yx}(x, y) & f_{yy}(x, y) \end{pmatrix}$$
$$= f_{xx}(x, y) f_{yy}(x, y) - [f_{xy}(x, y)]^2 .$$

- If $f_{xx}(a, b) > 0$ and $H_f(a, b) > 0$, then $f(a, b)$ is a relative minimum.

- If $f_{xx}(a, b) < 0$ and $H_f(a, b) > 0$, then $f(a, b)$ is a relative maximum.

- If $H_f(a, b) < 0$, then (a, b) is a saddle point.

- If $H_f(a, b) = 0$, then the test gives no information.

http://en.wikipedia.org/wiki/Second_partial_derivative_test

Sine and cosine values in quadrant I To convert the radian measures in the first row to degrees, simply multiply $180°/\pi$.

θ	0	$\pi/6$	$\pi/4$	$\pi/3$	$\pi/2$
$\cos\theta$	1	$\sqrt{3}/2$	$\sqrt{2}/2$	$1/2$	0
$\sin\theta$	0	$1/2$	$\sqrt{2}/2$	$\sqrt{3}/2$	1

Taylor's theorem Let f be a real-valued function defined on the closed interval $[a,b]$. Suppose $f^{(k)}$ is continuous on $[a,b]$ and $f^{(k+1)}$ exists everywhere on (a,b), where k is a positive integer. Then for each x and c in $[a,b]$ there is a z in (a,b) such that

$$f(x) = \frac{f^{(k+1)}(z)}{(k+1)!}(x-c)^{k+1} + \sum_{n=0}^{k} \frac{f^{(n)}(c)}{n!}(x-c)^n.$$

Hence, f can be approximated by the polynomial

$$\sum_{n=0}^{k} \frac{f^{(n)}(c)}{n!}(x-c)^n,$$

and we can estimate the error of our approximation by examining $\sup_{t\in(a,b)}|f^{(k+1)}(t)|$.

Uniform continuity Consider the metric spaces (X,ρ) and (Y,σ). A function $f: X \to Y$ is uniformly continuous on $U \subseteq X$ if and only if for all $\varepsilon > 0$ there is a $\delta > 0$ such that

$$\sigma\left(f(x_1), f(x_2)\right) < \varepsilon \quad \text{whenever} \quad \rho(x_1, x_2) < \delta,$$

for all x_1 and x_2 in U.

Uniform convergence theorem Suppose $\{f_n\}$ is a sequence of continuous functions that converge point-wise to the function f. If $\{f_n\}$ converges uniformly to f on an interval S, then f is continuous on S. See http://en.wikipedia.org/wiki/Uniform_convergence.

Work Let $C := \{\boldsymbol{\gamma}(t) : a \leq t \leq b\}$, where $\boldsymbol{\gamma} : \mathbb{R} \to \mathbb{R}^3$ is differentiable in each coordinate. Then the work done by a vector field $\boldsymbol{F}$ over C is

$$W = \int_C \boldsymbol{F} \cdot d\boldsymbol{\gamma} = \int_a^b \boldsymbol{F} \cdot \boldsymbol{\gamma}'(t)\, dt.$$

Made in the USA
Lexington, KY
15 September 2015